Smart answers
&
bad jokes

from a priest who proves
God has a sense of humor

Fr. Joe Krupp

Copyright 2009 FAITH Catholic

All rights reserved. No part of this publication may be reproduced, stored in a retrieval system, or transmitted, in any form or by any means, electronic, mechanical, photocopying, recording, or otherwise, without the written prior permission of FAITH Catholic, 1500 E. Saginaw St., Lansing, MI 48906.

www.faithcatholic.com

International Standard Book Number (10): 0-9790747-1-1
International Standard Book Number (13): 978-0-9790747-1-4

Cover and text design by Janna Stellwag and Matthew Tiller, Faith Catholic
Edited by Elizabeth Solsburg, Ann Jacob and Marybeth Hicks

Printed and bound in the United States of America.

Library of Congress Cataloging-in-Publication Data
Krupp, Joseph J.

Smart answers & bad jokes from a priest who proves God has a sense of humor
Joseph J. Krupp.

ISBN 0-9790747-1-1 (pbk.)

Dedication

This publication is dedicated to the memory of Pope John Paul II – truly one of the greatest gifts God gave us in our lifetime. His teachings inspired me, and Jesus changed my life as a result of them. I don't know that I can articulate at this point the influence this blessed man of God had on me, but I know it has been great. I was blessed enough to have met him twice; I found myself unable to speak both times. For those of you who know me, that's about the only time that has happened. I'd call that a miracle.

Acknowledgments

Whenever I buy a book (and bookstores in my area thank me for putting kids through college with my purchases), I always go to this part. I read the author's acknowledgments, and if there is a foreword, I gobble that up, too. As long as I can do this without getting a hard stare from the clerks in the bookstore, I'll read these to see if I actually want to buy the book.

I want to know something about the author. I want to decide if the author is someone I can support. To my mind, reading the manner in which an author thanks his family, friends and co-workers says much about the person.

After sneaking a peak at thousands of author acknowledgments, I confess I never thought I'd be writing one myself. Or if I ever imagined authoring a book, I guess I figured it would be like Christ's return – it'll happen eventually, but it's a long, long way off.

The truth is, I didn't set out to write a book. Instead, I wrote a series of columns for *Faith Magazine* that accumulated over time, until it seemed like a good idea to collect them in one place and publish them.

Oddly enough, I both love writing the column and fear it. On the one hand, it's fun to hunt down the writings of the church and discover new connections between our long history and the issues we struggle with in today's culture.

I fear it because I'm fallible, and frankly, a bit ditzy. When my fingers hit the keyboard, there's always a chance I'll mess up and really confuse folks!

Whenever I receive Communion, I ask God to help me stay faithful to his teachings – and I mean it. What if I mess it all up? There always will be a part of me convinced that when I die, the first words of Jesus at judgment will be, "Well, your heart was in the right place ..." Heck, even when I get it right, I know I'm still not doing justice to the truth.

The priest who lives with me is used to seeing me in front of the Blessed Sacrament with my Mac on my lap, surrounded by the catechism and about 10 other books mumbling "Poor Jesus." All I can do is try to let go of my fear, be as faithful as I can be and love Jesus with my whole heart.

I've seen this notion in other author's acknowledgments and now I know why ... it's something I feel compelled to say: Anything I got right is because of prayer and divine intervention, while whatever I may have got wrong is all my fault and probably the result of writing while watching my beloved Detroit Lions on TV.

My humble thanks to:

Jesus and His Bride; I still can't believe you let me be a priest. Thank you, thank you, thank you.

Mom and Dad: Because of you, I know Jesus. Is there anything better to say than that? Thanks for being my safe place and my sounding board, and for understanding why I hardly ever make it home.

My brothers and sisters: Laure, I don't know anyone who gets hit as hard as you, gets up as many times as you and still shines so beautifully. You are the best person I know. Paul, thanks for being my protective big brother and for how you love me. Edie, you are calm in every storm and you have a hot tub ... what could be better?

Heidi, you are so faithful, I just love how you follow Jesus. Kelly, you make everything beautiful; the world is better because of you. Jesse, you let the big Teutonic German call you his little bro; I feel safe with you. I just love you all so much.

All my nephews and nieces, you are a huge blessing in my life. Your uncle loves you very much.

Father Geoff Rose, our friendship is absolute proof that God simply must have a sense of humor. You're the best friend I could have.

Patrick O'Brien: Back at The Irish Pub, you knew my little "In the Know" column in the St. Gerard Parish bulletin could be a success. Thanks for your confidence and your vision.

Father John Klein: Besides being the best priest in the diocese, this column was your idea.

Mary M. (6:30 am Mass, right side, second to last pew), you named this column, so thanks to you, too.

Marybeth Hicks, Ann Jacob and Elizabeth Solsburg: My head is a scary little place, so thanks for going there and working so hard to make the column a book. Your edits make me look good (or at least better).

My brother priests in the Diocese of Lansing, Bishop Earl Boyea, Bishop Carl Mengeling and the late Bishop Kenneth Povish ... your examples inspire me.

Sacred Heart Seminary in Detroit: The fact that I went there should never cloud the truth that it is the best seminary in the country.

Lansing Catholic High School: Students, I love you and hope I served you well. Faculty and staff, you could be anywhere else making a lot more money and you stay and serve; I love you all for that.

In July 2009, I was assigned to the MSU campus as their new chaplain. I'm so grateful for how you've all welcomed and loved me. I'm proud of my "conversion" ... it's all because of you! Go Green!

Mt. Zion Catholic Pastoral Center is my spiritual home and inspiration. Thank you for teaching me to love and to evangelize.

Table of Contents

Questions about God .... Chapter 1

... and Jesus, the Holy Spirit, the Trinity, the Blessed Virgin, the Communion of Saints and the spiritual realm (whatever that is).

15 .... Does God make evil happen? If God created everything, did he create evil? What does God choose and what does God allow? What was the point of the crucifixion – was it necessary?

17 .... Why did God let Jesus suffer and die? Why does he seem to want us to suffer, too?

18 .... Where was Jesus' soul during the three days he was in the tomb?

19 .... Did Jesus raise himself from the dead?

20 .... Why did Jesus get baptized? He didn't have original sin, did he?

21 .... Did Jesus own the coat he wore? The church seems to own a lot of gold, art, property; why don't we sell all that and give it to the poor? Why do any of us own anything?

22 .... What exactly IS the Holy Spirit?

24 .... The Bible calls Jesus Mary's "firstborn son." *(Luke 2:7)* Did she have other children? Also, does it mention anywhere in the Bible when and how Joseph died?

25 .... Does every saint have a feast day? Who determines which saints' feast days make it on the calendar and which do not? It seems like every year the same saints are represented, some of whom seem rather "minor" (not to be judgmental).

26 .... Why do we pray to saints and have devotions? My non-Catholic friends say faith shouldn't be so complicated.

27 .... What is the deal with God and science? I hear all kinds of questions about the two, and everybody seems to contradict each other. What is the truth?

28 .... Why does God answer some prayers in the way the person wants them to be answered, and not others?

Table of Contents

Questions about the church . . . . Chapter 2
... what's up with the rules and regulations, and why does it seem so complicated to be Catholic?

31 . . . . What is the most important thing we believe as Catholics?

32 . . . . I am a Protestant who goes to church with my Catholic spouse. I want to receive Communion, but was told I can't. Why can't I?

33 . . . . I am a divorced Catholic. Some people have told me that I cannot receive Communion and others have said I can. Who is right?

34 . . . . Why can I go to Communion at some churches and not at others? Is there a rule here?

35 . . . . I recently attended a non-Catholic worship service where they recited the creed! What is up with that? They even said "I believe in one, holy, catholic and apostolic church." I don't get it. Help!

35 . . . . Does the church believe that only Catholics can go to heaven? I read something in the newspaper about the church publishing a document that says exactly that.

36 . . . . I have a friend who is Protestant and who is constantly telling me that our beliefs about heaven, hell and especially purgatory are not biblical. I looked, and she is right. It's not in the Scriptures. Why do we believe that if it's not in the Bible?

39 . . . . What does the church teach about cremation? What happens to us when we die? Do we believe in reincarnation?

41 . . . . Am I sinning if I am supposed to keep the Sabbath day holy, but I go to work?

41 . . . . What is devotionalism? My priest said it is a bad thing, but some of my fellow parishioners disagree. What's the truth here?

42 . . . . Why should I be confirmed? What does it mean to be an "active member of the church"?

43 . . . . My daughter is bringing her boyfriend home for the holidays and insists on sleeping in the same room with him. I'm opposed to that. What should I do?

44 . . . . Why should I go to a priest to talk about marriage when a priest doesn't have any experience in marriage?

Table of Contents

45 .... Why does the church require nine months of preparation before marriage? If couples feel they are ready, why is the church making them wait?

46 .... When priests sin, are they judged more harshly by God?

47 .... The priest who baptized my children left the priesthood under some very bad circumstances. Should I have my children re-baptized?

48 .... If I am saved through my baptism, then why do I need to go to a priest for confession?

49 .... What is the problem with general absolution – going to confession in a large group?

50 .... In churches, why did they remove the tabernacle from the main sanctuary to a spot to the side? Why are we hiding Jesus away?

51 .... There are many different religions out there and everybody thinks theirs is right. One of my friends says we are all right. Is it true that all religions are right?

52 .... What are the holy days of obligation and what does it mean when we have one?

53 .... What gives the church the authority to determine what is right and wrong? As far as I know, there is nothing on birth control, capital punishment, genetic engineering and/or cloning in the Bible. Doesn't it just hurt the credibility of the church when it is wrong (i.e., Galileo)?

55 .... What's so great about the priesthood? Why did you decide to become a priest?

56 .... Why is pride a sin – what about pride in your work or family? Is there a good kind of pride? If so, what kind of pride is sinful?

57 .... Some people say God will bless you with money if you live right. They also say it's the devil's fault if you live in poverty. Is this true?

58 .... Is it a sin to have stuff? In the Gospels, Jesus seems to imply we should give it all to the poor. But then everyone would be poor. What is really being asked of us?

60 .... I am troubled by a recent discovery. I saw in the news that a burial box (called an ossuary) was found that says Jesus had a brother. Is this true?

61 .... Why does the church seem so judgmental?

Table of Contents

62 .... Is organ donation OK for Catholics? If yes, why? Doesn't the Bible say that our bodies rise from the dead? What about dividing up a potential saint for relics?

63 .... Books such as *The Da Vinci Code* suggest the existence of writings that the church works hard to suppress. Are there other "gospels" such as the "Gnostic gospels?" What are they? Are they for real?

66 .... I have a Protestant friend who tells me Catholics only have nine commandments and we leave out the commandment about idols. She showed me in her Bible how we left it out. Is that true? Also, why do we have statues in churches if God says not to do it?

68 .... What do people mean when they ask if I am "born again?" I've always been Catholic — do I need to have a conversion experience and what would that look and feel like?

69 .... I've seen TV evangelists lay hands on people to "heal" them. How is this different from our sacrament of anointing the sick?

70 .... Why is there a need for the papacy?

70 .... What is papal infallibility and when is it invoked?

71 .... How does the church choose bishops?

72 .... What is the difference between Catholic Communion and Protestant Communion? May I receive Communion in a Protestant church?

74 .... How do people who are allergic to wheat receive Communion?

75 .... If I don't like my priest, can I switch parishes?

75 .... My friend's mom can speak in tongues and sometimes demonstrates this for us. It seems pretty weird and I'm not sure I believe it's anything other than gibberish. What's the deal with that?

76 .... What is a "charismatic" Catholic?

77 .... Is there such a thing as an "orthodox" Catholic (as opposed to Greek Orthodox)? I gather it's a term that implies people are "conservative" Catholics. I heard someone use this expression, but I didn't know there were different degrees or versions of Catholicism.

79 .... Did the priest scandals prove a celibate priesthood is unrealistic?

81 .... Is yoga a religion? Can you do yoga and be Catholic?

Table of Contents

82 . . . . Do people go right to heaven or wait until the end of time?

84 . . . . What happened to "limbo"?

86 . . . . Can I use Ouija boards, crystals and enneagrams?

88 . . . . Can I believe in Wicca and still be Catholic? I think I can since Wicca honors nature. What do you think?

Questions about relationships, emotions, and values . . . . Chapter 3

... exploring the tough job of getting along with others. Oy.

91 . . . . There's a couple at church who live together, but are not married. Is it my responsibility to tell them they cannot receive Communion? Should I alert the pastor to this situation?

93 . . . . I am really confused about forgiveness. I know we are supposed to forgive everyone, but does that mean I have to stay in the relationship? My marriage counselor is telling me something different. Please help.

95 . . . . I can't seem to get my grandson to go to church. His parents aren't taking him and I would really like him to go. What should I do?

96 . . . . I'm in high school. How can I defend the Catholic faith? I'm not sure I know enough to argue with non-believers or non-Catholics, even though I know our faith stands for the truth.

98 . . . . What does it mean to be pure in heart?

98 . . . . In a world that corrupts the innocence of children so completely, what can I do to keep my child pure?

100 . . . . When does sharing information become gossip?

100 . . . . When should you confront someone with the truth?

101 . . . . I keep quiet about things going on in my life because everything I say gets spread around. What should I do?

102 . . . . I feel guilty about putting my mother in a nursing home. Am I failing to honor her by doing this? How do I make this decision?

104 . . . . One of my brothers says he is no longer Catholic. He and his wife seem to spend a great deal of time criticizing my family and the Catholic Church. He says we aren't going to

# Table of Contents

	heaven. It's really hard at family gatherings because he is always trying to convert people. What should I do?
106	I am quite angry at some people at our parish over decisions they have made in our church. I am angry and I am hurt. What should I do?
107	My parents are trying to stop me from hanging out with some friends from school. I think they are judging them without getting to know them. What do you think?
109	I caught my boyfriend talking to his old girlfriend. I'm really jealous. I know this isn't a good thing, but how do I handle it?
110	My boyfriend won't let me talk to my friends anymore and wants me to quit activities he's not in. Is this normal?
111	What do I do if a friend is suicidal?
113	My brother has totally distanced himself from our parents. He keeps in touch with a couple of siblings, but his behavior toward our folks has created tension in our large family. How can we handle this without getting in the middle of a family meltdown?
115	I'm a woman in my late 30s. The chances of me getting married at this point appear to be slim and none. I'm sick of people asking me why I'm not married – it doesn't seem to occur to them that I would be if I'd fallen in love and someone had asked me! I'm already struggling with the fact that God hasn't seen fit to send me someone to spend my life with.

Questions about issues of the day . . . . . Chapter 4

… politics, sex and religion - three subjects we're supposed to avoid …
Notice how much time we spend talking about them?

117	What's so bad about being gay? What about gay marriage? I know some gay couples who are more committed to healthy, lifelong relationships than many heterosexual couples. Isn't there some hypocrisy in the church on this issue?
119	Do you give to the panhandler? I feel guilty walking by someone, but I'm afraid giving money just perpetuates the problem.
121	Why is the church so opposed to euthanasia? Why is it wrong to alleviate suffering? It seems to me we demand more compassion for a suffering dog than a person.

Table of Contents

123 .... How should we look at the war on terror? I am not clear on our role as "peacemaker" when we are fighting. What is peace?

125 .... Is it a sin to join the military if the war is unjust?

126 .... Can I be a conscientious objector?

126 .... Should we really be celebrating holidays such as Christmas when so much of the world is at war or otherwise suffering?

128 .... I have to make a decision between sending my child to Catholic school, which would involve me going back to work full time, and staying home with my younger children who are not in school yet. What do I do?

129 .... Since it's not likely the U.S. is going to outlaw abortion, why does the church make such a big deal out of it? Shouldn't every child be wanted and loved?

131. .... I'm thinking of going into politics someday. Am I obligated to assure that my political opinions all reflect the church's teaching exactly? What if I disagree about something such as abortion or the use of our military?

133. .... I always feel so much pressure at Christmas time. There's so much that has to be done and I have to make sure I get the right gift for each person. How can I balance my perspective so that Christmas is the prayerful experience it is meant to be?

134 .... At work, they are replacing people with machines. Is that moral?

136 .... What's the problem with software piracy? If it's possible to do it, why is it wrong? After all, Microsoft has billions – it's pretty much a victimless act.

137 .... Are any great scientists Christians?

138 .... Thinking back on the TV coverage of Hurricane Katrina, the media showed a lot of people stealing from stores and other places. Given the circumstances, was that OK?

139 .... How do I witness to my Catholic faith without being called a Jesus freak?

Chapter 1
Questions about God

My buddy Will and I were discussing what we wanted done when we died. I want an inscription on my tombstone that reads, "Pardon me for not getting up." I thought that was pretty funny until Will told me he wants T-shirts distributed at his funeral that say, "Will died and all I got was this lousy T-shirt." (Somehow, I don't see either of those things actually happening.)

Dear Fr. Joe,
Does God make evil happen? If God created everything, did he create evil? What does God choose and what does God allow? What was the point of the crucifixion – was it necessary?

OK, bunches of yummy questions to get us going; the first three are similar so I'll talk about them together – let's go:

First, does God make evil happen?

For starters, we need to agree on a definition of evil. Evil is a lack of good. Think of it like a glass of water. Optimist and pessimist jokes aside, we do define whether something is a glass of water by how much water it has; the more water you take out, the less accurate it is to call it a glass of water. In the same way, the more good we take out of a situation, the more evil it is. So, did God create evil? No – evil isn't something, it is a lack of something. Take that apart in your mind for a bit and see if it helps.

Second, what was the point of the crucifixion; was it necessary?

Absolutely. Let's take a look at our ***Catechism of the Catholic Church (CCC), sections 599 and 601:***

> *Jesus' violent death was not the result of chance in an unfortunate coincidence of circumstances, but is part of the mystery of God's plan .... (CCC 599)*
>
> *The Scriptures had foretold this divine plan of salvation through the putting to death of "the righteous one, my Servant" as a mystery of universal redemption, that is, as the ransom that would free men from the slavery of sin. (CCC 601)*

See, when our first parents sinned, their actions introduced sin and death into the world. They made, quite literally, a deal with the devil. In this deal, the devil promised them that they would be like God. All they had to do to get this life was disobey God. Adam and Eve agreed to this deal and "handed over the reins" to the devil. Sin and death came into the world, as well as the ability to choose right and wrong. Because of this decision, the law was born. The law basically gave people a list of what was the right thing to do and what was the wrong thing to do.

The problem with the law was, and is, that it only addresses the actions of people and not their hearts. Plus, it encourages arrogance, because, as it turns out, it is quite possible to follow the law perfectly and claim you are righteous all on your own. You can see yourself as obeying God and yet treat people with contempt! Anyone who works in the church can tell you of brushes with people who understand, know and follow the law, yet treat people in a way that is completely unacceptable.

Now, since the law became, in the words of Paul, a trap – and only worsened the cycle of sin – Jesus entered the picture. A key component to the story of Jesus is his death.

Jesus' death came in part as a result of his "yes" to God. He cried out in the garden, "Not my will but yours be done." *(Lk 22:42)* This is in contrast to us. Adam and Eve chose a way the devil assured them would lead to a divine life, but really only led to death. Jesus, by saying "yes" to death, trumped that disobedience and ushered in the possibility of life for us all.

WOW!

Jesus didn't just die for us though; he also rose for us. His death made possible the resurrection. His resurrection transformed us. Look at **Romans 6**; Paul reminds us that our sinful nature (the one given to us by the legacy of Adam and Eve) has been put to death by Jesus. When Jesus rose, he restored in us the freedom of the children of God.

So, did Jesus need to die? Yes. His death put our sinful natures to death. Jesus also needed to rise, to restore our nature to God's goodness and grace. Jesus' obedience even unto death trumped our disobedience in the quest for false life.

Jesus' death also made possible his resurrection, which gave us new, transformed hearts of flesh. Blessed be the name of the Lord.

Chapter One: Questions about God

Dear Fr. Joe,
Why did God let Jesus suffer and die? Why does he seem to want us to suffer, too?

We know of the awesome and wonderful power of our God. This is the same God who created the heavens and the earth and all that is in them and set it all in place. The Bible says we are "fearfully and wonderfully made" by the hand of God. He rules all of time and creation. There is no questioning his power. Yet why does God permit suffering and why did he allow Jesus to suffer?

God did the unexpected. He humbled himself. He took flesh and walked among us. God the Creator gave his creation power over himself and we put him to death. That act was the ultimate act of self-sacrifice and it is one we must imitate. This act of self-sacrifice is the one we celebrate each time we join in the Liturgy.

It is actually quite simple: If we wish to be Christian, we must imitate Christ, who sacrificed so much for us. This imitation of Christ's sacrifice is a challenge to each of us. It is, at times, a painful and difficult thing. When we experience that pain, we must always turn again to the example of Jesus who wept in the Garden of Olives. *(Mt 26:36-46)*

Because God became human, he knows our pain. He knows what it is like to lose a friend to death, or fear, or even betrayal. He has been there, done that and offers now to walk with us when our self-sacrifice leads to suffering. But we also know it does not end there. Jesus rose from the dead and promises us that "if we die with (him), we shall rise with (him)." In the words of one of our deacons at St. Gerard, "Can you imagine how Jesus felt when he came out of the tomb?"

No kidding! That is the way we can feel, too. When we sacrifice ourselves (what we want or think we need) and something in us has to die, we can count on the Lord, who is faithful and true to restore us to life.

So, why did Jesus have to die?

Well, someone had to. Sounds bad? It's true! The price of sin entering the world is death. Before Jesus, believers used to offer animal sacrifices of lambs to God for their sins. These lambs would have to be without mark or stain or blemish and they were offered to God as a sacrifice for sins.

Another way to expiate sins before Jesus was to bring a goat into the center of the community. Each person would lay their hands on the goat and whisper their sins. When all were finished, they would send the goat off into the wilderness to die. (This, by the way, is where we get the term "scapegoat.")

Jesus came as the spotless lamb. He never sinned and he offered himself up by taking upon himself the sins of the whole world through all of time and history. His pure, sinless blood brought forgiveness for all time and all people.

Let's celebrate the mystery of our faith: "Christ has died, Christ is risen, Christ will come again!"

Warning! Bad joke ahead!

A young executive was leaving the office late one evening when he found the CEO standing in front of a shredder with a piece of paper in his hand.

"Listen," said the CEO, "this is a very sensitive and important document here, and my secretary has gone for the night. Can you make this thing work for me?" "Certainly," said the young executive. He turned the machine on, inserted the paper, and pressed the start button.

"Excellent, excellent!" said the CEO, as his paper disappeared inside the machine. "I just need one copy..."

Dear Fr. Joe,
Where was Jesus' soul during the three days he was in the tomb?

Strangely enough, we think at least some of those days, he was in Toledo ... who knew? Seriously, though, the **catechism** directly addresses this in **sections 631-637**. I will summarize as best I can what is found there.

First, we need to understand that Jesus did, in fact, die. "... Jesus, like all men, experienced death, and in his soul joined the others in the realm of the dead." What happened to Jesus on Good Friday wasn't something akin to death, but actual death. That is important because of what that death allowed Jesus to do.

As the Son of God, he descended into death as the Savior, not just another person who died. The idea is this: That all death that occurred before the "Jesus event" led people to an afterlife called Sheol, where they were "deprived of the vision of God." This was the case for both the good and the bad who had died. However, we do know that the afterlife was different for the good and the bad, as is shown in the story of Lazarus. Jesus said Lazarus was at "Abraham's bosom," and the rich man was "in torment." *(Lk 16:19-31)*

So, before Jesus, everyone who died descended into Sheol; a place where they could not see God. The people who rejected God had a different experience there than those who followed and loved God. When Jesus died, he descended into that place and delivered those whom he knew loved and served God from Sheol into heaven. Remember, Jesus "did not descend into hell to deliver the damned, nor to destroy the hell of damnation, but to free the just who had gone before him." *(CCC 633)*

Dear Fr. Joe,
Did Jesus raise himself from the dead?

Let's start with Scripture on this one. First, **Romans 10:9:**

For, if you confess with your mouth that Jesus is Lord and believe in your heart that God raised him from the dead, you will be saved.

OK, here Paul shows us that God the Father raised Jesus from the dead. Now, let's look at **Romans 8:11**:

If the Spirit of the one who raised Jesus from the dead dwells in you, the one who raised Christ from the dead will give life to your mortal bodies also, through his Spirit that dwells in you.

Here, Paul tells us it was God the Holy Spirit who raised Jesus from the dead. But wait! There's more! Now, let's look at two passages from the **Gospel of John**. First, **John 2:18-21:**

At this the Jews answered and said to him, "What sign can you show us for doing this?" Jesus answered and said to them, "Destroy this temple and in three days I will raise it up." The Jews said, "This temple has been under construction for 46 years, and you will raise it up in three days?" But he was speaking about the temple of his body.

And **John 10:17-18:**

This is why the Father loves me, because I lay down my life in order to take it up again. No one takes it from me, but I lay it down on my own. I have power to lay it down, and power to take it up again. This command I have received from my Father.

When we read these passages, we see Jesus raising himself from the dead! So, which one was it?

It was all three – the wonder and the mystery of our triune God working to raise Jesus from the dead.

Dear Fr. Joe,
Why did Jesus get baptized? He didn't have original sin, did he?

No, Jesus didn't have original sin. In fact, he didn't need to be baptized, technically. So, why did he?

Let's look at the Scripture(s) where it happened and see why. The story of Jesus' baptism can be found in the following Gospels: ***Mark 1:9-11; Matthew 3:13-17; Luke 3:21-22.***

Before we jump into the Scripture itself, let's tackle a modern problem. I know there are some who will tell you these stories are made up to teach us a lesson. I don't buy it. I believe what the *catechism* states is true – the Gospel stories are accurate accounts of events in the life of Jesus as viewed by his disciples and handed on to us. This is a very important point to keep in mind while contemplating the baptism of Jesus.

OK, back to the four Gospels and the accounts of Jesus' baptism by John. What do all of these stories have in common? First, the descent of the Holy Spirit upon Jesus. The Holy Spirit, in the form of a dove, was a witness to the people who were watching. It wasn't because Jesus needed the Holy Spirit – it was a message to those who were watching that Jesus carried within himself the power and blessings of God. The dove was a sign of peace and salvation (the story of Noah, remember?) and its appearance would have been a great sign to the people of war-torn Israel.

Second, and my favorite part, is the voice from heaven. God's voice stated: "This is my beloved Son in whom I am well pleased." Wow! What power in that statement!

My good friend, Paul Dull, always points out to me, "Father, God could have taken that moment to explain things theologically. I know I would have. But God didn't. He paused and said what any good dad says: 'That's my boy! I love him!'" Can you imagine that? I've had some experience of that on the sidelines at high school football games. Beaming dads and moms would nudge me and say, "Did you see my son out there?"

Can you see God that way? Close your eyes, turn off the noise around you and hear the voice of God echoing from the pages of the Gospel, pointing you out to the world and saying, "This is my beloved son!" or "This is my beloved daughter!" We must hear that voice because, like Jesus, we have been baptized. At our baptism, we were joined with Jesus in a bond that cannot be broken. Remember – God doesn't change his mind.

Warning! Bad joke ahead!

A friend of mine recently sent me a list of bulletin bloopers. I thought I'd share one with you. This announcement supposedly appeared in a local bulletin: "Our youth basketball team is back in action against Christ the King Baptist this Wednesday at 8 p.m. in the recreation hall. Come out and watch us clobber Christ the King."

Dear Fr. Joe,

Did Jesus own the coat he wore? The church seems to own a lot of gold, art, property; why don't we sell all that and give it to the poor? Why do any of us own anything?

Great questions. Did Jesus own the coat he wore? Absolutely. But maybe I can suggest that a better question would be "Did Jesus' coat own him?" The answer to that would be a resounding "no." The key to possessions is that we own them and they don't own us.

How do we know if that is the case? The first step to knowing if we own something or if it owns us is to break everything we have into two categories: wants and needs.

Wants are things that are there for our enjoyment or pleasure. They bring us a small measure of happiness, but ultimately, they are not things that we must have. I think my sanity is an example of this.

Needs are those things that are important for our survival, or enable us to function in the world. Great examples are my truck and phone – I need these to effectively function as a priest. A serious argument could be made that Double Stuf Oreos® are essential to my survival, but I won't go there.

In terms of wants, we should be willing and able to part with them at a moment's notice to help someone who will use our help responsibly. If we can do that, then we own our possessions and they don't own us.

Your next question is one a lot of people ask, and I am glad I finally have a chance to address it here. The church does own a vast storehouse of art and treasures; one look at the Vatican Museum or St. Peter's Basilica can absolutely take your breath away. The sheer beauty of those collections is amazing.

But here is the thing – did you notice that I typed, "One look at?" That is the key – anyone can see and admire these treasures whenever they are on display. The Vatican doesn't collect any kind of wealth for and from them – they are available to view at the Vatican, and then often travel to museums around the world. The church acts as guardian of the beauty that various artists have created through the ages.

Jesus' words stand true:

The poor you will always have with you. (Mt 26:11)

Incidentally, he said this in response to his disciples when they objected to a woman pouring expensive oil on his body. They thought she should have sold the oil and given the money to the poor. But Jesus told them that there was nothing wrong with her lavishing this expensive oil on him. In the same way, there is nothing wrong with people donating gold and precious items to adorn a beautiful church building, since this is done to the glory of God.

Make sure and take a look at the ***catechism, sections 2501 and 2502.***

They give us a great description of the beauty and power of art.

Warning! Bad joke ahead!

Two questions to ponder:
Q: What kind of man was Boaz before he married?
A: Ruthless.
Q: Who was the greatest financier in the Bible?
A: Noah. He was floating his stock while everyone else was in liquidation.

Dear Fr. Joe,
What exactly IS the Holy Spirit?

Did you ever try to define love? It's tough, isn't it? It's often easier to describe the effects of love than to try to nail down the word itself. Well, it's the same with the Holy Spirit. But, being the "Question and Answer Man," I shall attempt to do both. So, without further ado, let's plunge into looking at who the Holy Spirit is and what the Holy Spirit does.

Let's start with the ***catechism***, shall we? The ***catechism*** refers to the Holy Spirit as being a few things:

First of all, the Holy Spirit is the third person of the Trinity – the love of the Father for the Son and the Son for the Father. The love of the Father and the Son for each other is so intense that it is a person: the Holy Spirit. This Holy Spirit then is a Spirit of Love. The Holy Spirit is coequal with the Father and the Son and is their love personified.

The Holy Spirit is also the advocate. An advocate is like a lawyer or a defender who speaks for us. This is what the Holy Spirit does. In fact, without the Holy Spirit, we would not even be able to pray (not that we don't try, though!). Our first step when we pray should not be to inundate God with as many words as possible, but instead to pause, take a deep breath and ask the Spirit to pray through us. I use a simple prayer my mother taught me: "Holy Spirit, rise up in me and pray." This will help our prayer life tremendously, because it is not about our effort but our openness to the Spirit! What a gift God has given us in the Spirit – he requires prayer from us, and then gives us the means to pray!

Now, we are going to take a different tack. We are going to look at SOME of the ways the Spirit has shown itself in the Scriptures. The first chapters of the first book of the Bible contain this message:

> *The Lord God formed man out of the clay of the ground and blew into his nostrils the breath of life. (Gn 2:7)*

Those are references to the Holy Spirit and the word used is Ruah, which loosely means "the breath of God." One of the earliest understandings we have of the Holy Spirit is that of God's breath.

Jumping to the Gospels, we see some radical miracles on the part of Jesus. How did he do it? The Holy Spirit. It was the Holy Spirit that raised Jesus from the dead, gave sight to the blind man and expelled demons. It was through the Holy Spirit that Jesus was able to say what he said and do what he did.

While that is interesting, here is what is truly awe-inspiring: Jesus gave the Holy Spirit to us!

> *And when he had said this, he breathed on them and said to them, "Receive the holy Spirit. Whose sins you forgive are forgiven them, and whose sins you retain are retained." (Jn 20: 22-23)*

Jesus gave the disciples the Holy Spirit so that they could forgive sins on earth. This has two direct effects on us. First of all, this is how the sacrament of reconciliation works. When you step into the confessional, that moment is brought to you by the Holy Spirit! I know, it sounds like a commercial. In fact, I wanted priests to wear a patch on their clothing that served as an advertisement for the Holy Spirit, but the bishop said "no." All my good ideas get shot down.

You need more? No problem! Look at the **Book of Acts**: Jesus is risen from the dead, the disciples have seen him, yet they still hide in an upper room. They have the desire and love to follow and die for Jesus, but they don't yet have the courage until the Holy Spirit comes. After the arrival of the Holy Spirit, they are all over the known world preaching the Gospel and handing it down to us. Each one of those disciples died terrible and violent deaths rather than forsake Jesus. Their past mistakes show us it wasn't just a matter of their desire; that desire failed them when Jesus was led away to be killed. No, it was the Holy Spirit who helped them, gave them the strength to do what Jesus called them to do.

Warning! Bad joke ahead!

I heard a great story the other day about two judges who were in an accident. They were both speeding and the arriving police officer informed them that they had to go to court. So, they decided, why not try each other? They quickly found an empty courtroom and started. The first judge got up and said, "Well, I have reviewed the facts of the case and fine you $1." The second judge nodded, took his seat and said, "I have reviewed the facts of this case and fine you $750." The first judge was flabbergasted! "I fined you a dollar and you do this? What's going on?"

The second judge said, "You don't understand; this is becoming quite a problem. Why, this is the second case of speeding we've heard of today!"

Dear Fr. Joe,

The Bible calls Jesus Mary's "firstborn son." (Luke 2:7) Did she have other children? Also, does it mention anywhere in the Bible when and how Joseph died?

OK, your question basically has two parts. Let's take the first one first. (How's that for prioritizing?)

"Firstborn" was a significant title in Scriptural times. As Jews, there were laws and prescriptions that Mary and Joseph followed for Jesus' dedication that are in line with the firstborn male son. *(cf. Luke 2:23)*

It doesn't mean that Mary had other children. It just means Jesus was the first male born to her.

In terms of Joseph's death, I quote Samuel Clemens, who said, "I quote others to express myself better." Thus, I will give you the section from the **Catholic Encyclopedia** on that one:

> *This is the last we hear of St. Joseph in the sacred writings, and we may well suppose that Jesus' foster-father died before the beginning of the Savior's public life. In several circumstances, indeed, the Gospels speak of the latter's mother and brothers (Mt 12:46; Mk 3:31; Lk 8:19; Jn 7:3), but never do they speak of His father in connection with the rest of the family; they tell us only that Our Lord, during His public life was referred to as the son of Joseph (Jn 1:45; 6:42; Lk 4:22) the carpenter (Mt 13:55). Would Jesus, moreover, when about to die on the Cross, have entrusted His mother to John's care, had St. Joseph been still alive? According to the apocryphal "Story of Joseph the Carpenter," the holy man reached his 111th year when he died, on 20 July (A. D. 18 or 19). St. Epiphanius gives him 90 years of age at the time of his demise; and if we are to believe the Venerable Bede, he was buried in the Valley of Josaphat. In truth we do not know when St. Joseph died; it is most unlikely that he attained the ripe old age spoken of by the "Story of Joseph" and St. Epiphanius. The probability is that he died and was buried at Nazareth.*

Warning! Bad joke ahead!

I was sitting in a restaurant looking over the menu. The waiter came over and I asked, "Sir, how do you prepare the chicken?" He paused and said, "Nothing special really. We just tell them, 'Look, you're going to die.'"

Dear Fr. Joe,
Does every saint have a feast day? Who determines which saints' feast days make it on the calendar and which do not? It seems like every year the same saints are represented, some of whom seem rather "minor" (not to be judgmental).

Alrighty then! Let's go with No. 2 first, because Jesus said "the first will be last and the last will be first." Just tryin' to be Scriptural.

Anyway, the church decides which saints' feast days make it on the calendar and which ones don't. This can be done in two ways. In the first way, popular devotion over a period of time can lead the church to officially recognize it. In the second way, sometime during or shortly after a saint is canonized, the church will ask us to celebrate the saint and his or her contributions on a specific day. I would assume that the ones chosen to be on the calendar are those who address, in some way, issues that are timeless.

There are saints who address issues that are no longer as important as others. For example, if a saint spent his or her life defending the fact that Jesus is the Son of God then that would be something that is timeless – meaning that people always seem to attack that teaching. If they taught us about the benefits or evils of the crossbow (and there really is a saint that did that!), then that might not be something we need to focus on as much.

Does every saint have a feast day? Yes and no (I really should run for office).

Yes, because of All Saints Day, on which we honor all of the saints who are on the calendar, along with those who are not. No, because there are only so many days in the year and at last count there were more than 3,000 recognized and canonized saints.

Warning! Bad joke ahead!

So, there I was sitting in the confessional when a man came running in. He said: "Forgive me, Father, for I have sinned. I stole this turkey to feed my family. Would you take it and settle my guilt?"

"No, that's not the answer," I replied. "Why don't you return it to the one you stole it from?"

"I tried," he said, "but he refused. Oh, Father, what should I do?"

"Well, if you are telling the truth, then it is all right for you to keep it for your family."

The man thanked me and left. When confession was over, I went back into the rectory. Walking into the kitchen, I found that someone had stolen our turkey.

Dear Fr. Joe,
Why do we pray to saints and have devotions? My non-Catholic friends say faith shouldn't be so complicated.

Praying to saints is an important part of our Catholic tradition. A lot of people misunderstand why we pray to saints and it actually is not that hard to explain. I will take it step by step, with Scripture references attached, to explain why we pray to saints. Now, the Scripture reference may be for a quote, or for an idea. Check it out for yourselves and see if this helps:

First, we believe that some of those who die are in heaven *(I Jn 3:2, I Cor 13:12, Rv 22:4)*, some are in purgatory *(II Mc 12:46, I Cor 3:15, I Pt 1:7)* and some are in hell. *(I Jn 3:14-15)*

Of those, there are some whom we are SURE are in heaven. We look at their lives, their love for God and neighbor, and the fact that praying to them results in what Jesus calls "good fruit." *(Mt 25:31, I Cor 15:26-27, Eph 4:16)*

If someone is in heaven, they are perfectly united with Jesus. Like the apostle Paul, we believe that those who are dead in Christ are really alive. *(Phil 3:21, I Cor 15:44)* They are in heaven praising and worshiping God.

We who are alive and worship Jesus are also united with him, or as Scripture puts it, we are "taken up into his body." *(I Cor 6:13-15, 19-20, Col 2:12, 3:1)*

Since we are united with Christ through our baptism, we are also united with those who have died and are in heaven with the Lord. *(II Mc 12:45, Eph 4:1-6)*

It is proper for us to ask those who have been raised and are united with Jesus to pray for us.

Literally, for those who believe in the resurrection of the dead, asking someone who has died to pray for us is like asking our neighbor to pray for us – but even better.

Why? Because people in heaven understand God and his plan for us in a way we will not until we are raised up with Christ Jesus. They can take our prayers and refine them and make them more in accord with what Jesus wants.

In terms of devotions, then, we have stylized ways of praying to the saints. A format is always helpful in that regard, isn't it?

So, the next time you are needing God's guidance on something or in need of help, ask your friends to pray for you. The friends you can see and the friends you cannot.

Dear Fr. Joe,
What is the deal with God and science? I hear all kinds of questions about the two, and everybody seems to contradict each other. What is the truth?

Faith and science. Sometimes it seems we're crossing into enemy territory when we talk about the two. "Basic scientific research, as well as applied research, is a significant expression of man's dominion over creation. Science and technology are precious resources when placed at the service of man ... By themselves however; they cannot disclose the meaning of existence and of human progress." *(CCC 2293)* Good stuff comes from that ***catechism!***

The point is this: We are foolish if we try to live in faith at the expense of scientific knowledge. We are foolish if we ignore faith and worship science. Francis Bacon says, "A little science pulls man away from God. A lot of science brings him back." We have confidence in God and the fact that knowledge of his creation will point to him. The scientist who learns all he or she can is worshiping God, because knowledge of God's creation is knowledge of God. The *catechism* reminds us that science can take us only so far. In God alone does the human person find the meaning of life and progress. Jesus and his kingdom have to be at the center of what we learn for it to be truly worship.

Scientific findings are not threats to our faith; they are, instead, opportunities to discover more about this wonderful creation and about God. Let's not fight the inevitable or worship the unlikely. Instead, we can be a part of helping science and faith to join hands in worship of God.

Dear Fr. Joe,
Why does God answer some prayers in the way the person wants them to be answered, and not others?

That is a great question; it's going to take a "process" to answer it, so please stick with me as we get there.

First of all, we have to recognize that our faith in God is supposed to be a result of a relationship. Through our daily prayers and contact with God, we come to understand that our loving, all powerful God wants what is best for us. The words of the prophet Jeremiah become our lived experience, "For I know well the plans I have in mind for you, plans for your welfare, not your woe. Plans for a future full of hope." *(Jer 29:11)*

Just as our experiences with people can lead us to trust them, so our lived and growing experience with God can lead us to trust him. As we grow in our relationship, we naturally grow in trust.

One of the most important things we can learn about God is that there are some things God cannot do. Yes, you read right: There are things that God cannot do. One of them is that God cannot remove from us the "aftershocks" of sin. When we choose to sin, we must embrace the consequences. We can pray for God to walk with us through the difficulties and he will, but God cannot, or will not, remove the consequences of our bad choices. Now, this is not to say that all bad things that happen to us are our fault – that would be ludicrous.

So, what happens when we pray? When we pray, our souls are entering the presence of God and basking in his divine presence. As we stand in the light of God's glory, we are transformed and changed, even when we don't feel anything happening. It's like riding an exercise bike; it's not like we are getting anywhere geographically, but we do it because we know there are things going on inside us that we cannot see. Our hearts and bodies are growing stronger, muscles are tearing and rebuilding, the heart's capacity to handle stress is increasing, our lungs are growing stronger, etc. All these things are happening, even though we don't feel it.

Prayer works the same way. When we pray for a specific situation, we are being changed – our souls are being strengthened to handle the coming grief or our capacity for joy is being increased.

As we approach the wrap-up to this question, the element of mystery needs to be addressed. Whenever we talk about God, we are almost always giving our "best guess." God is not us. The Scriptures put it this way, "For my ways are not your ways, says the Lord." *(Is 55:8)*

Think of it this way – the way you and I experience life is limited by two things. First, we are only able to understand our lives in the context of our life and experience. We don't know how different actions and inactions on our part affect people all around us. Second, we are limited by how we view time. We see our lives like a scroll unfolding; God sees the whole of our lives, from beginning to end, in an eternal "now."

Warning! Bad joke ahead!

The other day at the mall, I was stopped and asked if I would participate in a survey. The question was, "What is the greatest invention of the last 500 years?" I said it was the telephone because of how we communicate. The guy next to me suggested it was the television because it brought us all out to the larger world. The third guy looked real thoughtful and then said, "The thermos. You see, yesterday, I put piping hot coffee in it and five hours later, it was still hot. Today, I put chilled milk in there and now, five hours later, it's still cold!" I didn't see his point until he added, "How the heck did it know the difference?" Oh, the wonders of being flexible!

Smart answers & bad jokes

Chapter 2
Questions about the church

A down-and-out musician was playing his guitar in the middle of a busy shopping mall. Striding over, a policeman asked, "May I please see your permit?"

"I don't have one," confessed the musician.

"In that case, you'll have to accompany me."

"Splendid!" exclaimed the musician. "What shall we sing?"

Dear Fr. Joe,
What is the most important thing we believe as Catholics?

Well, let's check the ***Catechism of the Catholic Church (CCC)***. Numbers ***232, 234 and 237*** call the Trinity the "Central Mystery of Our Faith." That little statement says a lot.

First, it is central to what we believe because of how the Trinity exists. What we believe as Catholics (and most Protestant denominations believe this, as well) is that you have three distinct persons who are somehow one and are literally spending their existence giving of their total selves to the other two. They hold nothing back in their love for one another and give until they should be empty. But they are never empty – the other members of the Trinity are filling them.

THAT is central to our faith because that is what our lives are to be as well: Giving all of our love, our life, our strength and, indeed, our very being to our Trinitarian God and his people who fill us with a love that we cannot comprehend because it's so vast. It's also called a "mystery" because we can never understand precisely how it happens.

Now, it's important to note that when the church says "mystery," it doesn't mean the same thing as a television mystery. It means, in the words of one of my teachers, "constantly revealing." We could literally spend our lives taking this apart and learning something new each day. That rocks! Think about it...

I remember distinctly an event that happened in one of my theology classes in seminary. The professor had just given a lecture on the Trinity – what it is, why it is, etc. We all shuffled in from our break for the second hour of the class and sat down, ready to take notes.

Our prof ran through the review of the previous hour and asked an important question: "So what?"

We paused for a moment. "This is theology! What does he mean, 'So what?'"

We waited for him to speak again. And he waited for us.

Then it occurred to me that theology and questions about the nature of God are supposed to evoke a response from us. Our beliefs about the Trinity are not just bits of knowledge that we try to grasp to get smarter. Instead, our knowledge and the learning processes that take us there are supposed to invade us, change us, force a response from us.

Everytime someone teaches you something about the church or what she believes, ask the big question – "So what?" Then see where it takes you. By doing this, we might find theology and faith moving from the category of "Spiritual Trivia" to "Life-Changing, In-Your-Face Truth." It's that good, folks, I promise.

Sometimes people come to me and say they feel bad because they are questioning their faith. I always try to encourage people that the church is precisely FOR those who have questions. We don't go to a doctor because we feel great, and we don't go to church because we have all the answers. We come to God because we realize we need something more. We come to God because we are sinners who need the unconditional love of Jesus so badly. We come to God because we rejoice in the fact that God can work even in the worst of us.

If God can take something as horrible as crucifixion and death and make it beautiful, think of what he can do with our questions and sinfulness.

Dear Fr. Joe,

I am a Protestant who goes to church with my Catholic spouse. I want to receive Communion but was told I can't. Why can't I?

To be honest, I am not sure why you would want to. You see, to Catholics, the Eucharist is the sign and source of our unity of belief and purpose. By receiving it, Catholics are affirming what we believe about our faith and receiving strength to live that belief. We believe that the host is the actual body of Christ, given to us through our church. We don't consider it a symbol of Christ, as would most Protestants, but the real thing *(please see John 6)*.

If you find that you agree with the church's position on this, you may want to talk to your husband's priest about becoming Catholic.

Otherwise, please know that you are always welcome to join us in worship. I personally find it inspiring and beautiful that you continue to join your spouse in worship. Thank you for your great example.

Warning! Bad joke ahead!

I was asked to do a census of the people who make up our parish community. During one of my visits, I knocked on a door and a young girl answered. Through the screen door, I asked if her mom or dad was home. She looked a little reluctant to answer the question, so I bent down and said, as innocently as possible, "Do you know who I am?" She immediately ran deeper into the house calling, "Mom! There's a man at the door who doesn't know who he is!" Oops!

Dear Fr. Joe,

I am a divorced Catholic. Some people have told me I cannot receive Communion and others have said I can. Who is right?

Me. Always. And write that down!

Well, about your specific question, though, you may be able to receive Communion. Let's run through the policies. First of all, a Catholic who is divorced and not remarried is able to receive Communion. It is those who are divorced and remarried outside of the church who are not permitted.

The reason is because the host that you receive – the body of Christ – is, among other things, a sign of our unity with each other, and the church as a whole. Those who are baptized are obligated to marry in the church, and marrying outside of the church breaks the unity that your parents, or you, promised at your baptism.

Warning! Bad joke ahead!

A man made pancakes for his two boys. He finished the first pancake and set it on the table. Unfortunately, the two immediately began fighting for control of that one pancake. Seeing an opportunity for learning, he stated (rather solemnly, I might add), "Boys, if Jesus were here he would say 'you take the first pancake.'" Stepping back, the father looked at his two boys who were deep in thought. The father was, happy to have prompted such mental gymnastics by his wisdom. Suddenly, the older boy grabbed the pancake, threw it on his plate and said to his younger sibling, "You get to be Jesus first." Now, THAT is what we call applying theology to everyday life.

Dear Fr Joe,
Why can I go to Communion at some churches and not at others? Is there a rule here?

Well, if you hearken back to my award-winning, earth-shattering answer about Communion and divorce, you will see my humble response there talks largely of the concept of "communion." Not the consecrated host, but rather our communion with other churches. What does it mean?

Well, as Roman Catholics, there are churches with whom we are in communion and some with whom we are not in communion. What determines communion? Communion is unity of belief and purpose. Usually issues of our communion with other churches have to do with authority and doctrine. When we say "authority," we usually mean the structure of the church, and when we say "doctrine," it has to do with what we believe. For example, as Roman Catholics, we believe that the pope is our spiritual head. He is the one who defines what authentic theology is and what is not. He always does this in union with Sacred Scripture and tradition; this is not something he can or does abuse. Any church that recognizes his supreme authority in matters of faith and morals, then, is in communion with us on issues of authority, and therefore on issues of doctrine. Because of that, you could probably receive Communion at those churches. Get it?

Now, walking down via the negative path, there are other churches with whom we are not in communion. Maybe they disagree with our system of authority, maybe they disagree with our theology; whatever it is, while we are one in Christ, we are not one in practice. Because of that, we do not pretend we are by receiving the sign of our unity. If we did, it would be like a single person wearing a wedding ring – it just isn't true!

Chapter Two: Questions about the church

Dear Fr. Joe,
I recently attended a non-Catholic worship service where they recited the creed! What is up with that? They even said "I believe in one, holy, catholic and apostolic Church." I don't get it. Help!

Fear not, oh distressed one, I shall come to your aid on this. The creed is a statement of what we hold as true, and you will find little dispute on some of the issues in many Christian churches over whom Jesus was and is, the role of the Trinity, etc. The church you were at would obviously then agree with the Roman Catholic Church on theological issues, and probably disagree over authority issues, the role of the pope, the need for a hierarchy, etc. So, they say the creed because they agree with it.

The phrase "one, holy, catholic and apostolic" is a little more simple. The word "catholic" (lower-case 'c') literally means "universal," or "all-encompassing." Those who say that phrase, then, agree with us on the issue of being "one, holy, universal and apostolic." So, just like us, they say what they believe!

Dear Fr. Joe,
Does the church believe that only Catholics can go to heaven? I read something in the newspaper about the church publishing a document that says exactly that.

Nope. The document to which you refer could easily be put under the category of "most misunderstood." This is a great question because it reminds us that as we study our beliefs, we shouldn't rely solely on the media for information.

So, what does this document, *Dominus Iesus*, say? Clearly, it is an attempt by the church to reiterate and clarify the Second Vatican Council's work in regard to the question of salvation for non-Catholics and non-Christians. The central idea? That Jesus Christ is the way to heaven. Only Jesus. We state this belief firmly in all we do and this is one thing about which we will not compromise or change.

Being nice is not enough. Being good is not enough. We can never get to the point where we earn salvation. Salvation is a gift that comes from God through the words and actions of Jesus. Look at your Bible. In the **Gospel of John** *(14:6)*, Jesus says, "I am the way, and the truth and the life. No one comes to the Father except through me."

So, does that mean non-Catholics go to hell? Or people who do not believe in Jesus? Nope again! Take a look at your ***Catechism of the Catholic Church, sections 836-848***. There, the church clearly breaks down its attitude toward "non-Christians." Be sure to check that out.

What is the idea, then? How do we say that no one is saved outside of Jesus and yet say that non-Christians can be holy people who we will see in heaven? Well, we go back to two things: First, there is the fact that all of us are God's children and form what the church calls "that one community that is the human family." Our common Creator connects us to one another. Second, we look at the act of Jesus on the cross. That perfect act is so powerful and lasting that it extends to all of creation. Put these two things together and you have the core of *Dominus Iesus*. Let's go step by step:

- We believe that our worship of Jesus on the cross, living for him and imitating him, is the way to salvation.
- Christians do this and are connected through our loving God to the rest of his children who love God, but don't know Jesus.
- These two realities combine to offer salvation to the whole world.

Whew! It wasn't easy to put all that together! There it is, though. Please, do not forget to pull out your ***Catechism of the Catholic Church*** and see what the church says specifically about non-Christians. If you do not have a ***catechism,*** try your local parish. It should have a copy for you.

Warning! Bad joke ahead!

I couldn't figure it out. It happened at least once a week. There I was in class, teaching, and my dog would walk in. I keep her in the office with the door shut while I teach, and I couldn't figure out how she got out and knew where I was. I couldn't figure out who was doing it. Then I saw it. No kidding folks – my dog can open doors. She uses her paws and opens the door. Now, how she always manages to go right to the room I am in still remains a mystery to me. Allow me to assure you, I DO shower, so it can't be that ...

Dear Fr. Joe,

I have a friend who is Protestant and who is constantly telling me that our beliefs about heaven, hell and especially purgatory are not biblical. I looked, and she is

right. It's not in the Scriptures. Why do we believe that if it's not in the Bible?

Great question! This really taps into two areas of our difference with our Protestant brothers and sisters, so we will take it one at a time. I need to point out that I have a limited amount of space here, and am not going to be able to cover this adequately enough for some. Please consult your *catechism* for the full blown discussion, particularly *sections 80-87*.

First, the "non-Biblical" issue. As Catholics, we do not believe that Scripture alone covers everything; we also believe that we need something we call "sacred tradition." Now, this tradition is not like "let's have turkey at Thanksgiving!" It's more than that. Sacred tradition is, in the words of the *catechism (81)*:

[the transmission] in its entirety [of] the Word of God which has been entrusted to the Apostles by Christ the Lord and the Holy Spirit.

Where do we get this authority?

From the handing on by the apostles of teachings that are not in Scripture. This also covers those teachings that come about as a result of modern issues.

Look at it this way: Where do Scriptures get their authority? Who decided what books "made the cut" into the Bible? Paul wrote other letters. Other Gospels were written. Who decided which ones were authentically from the apostles and which ones were written by others? Sacred tradition did. Sacred Scripture is a collection of books that the apostles and their successors said were consistent with what Jesus said and taught. These books have no authority if they are not recognized by the apostles and their successors. So, we used sacred tradition to tell us which books were divinely inspired and which books were not. Because of this, we cannot disregard sacred tradition without disregarding the authority of Scripture. As Catholics we embrace them both.

Let's look at what we believe about heaven, hell and purgatory. First of all, we believe that heaven, hell and purgatory all start here on earth. All three are natural consequences of our choices. Catholics believe God always respects the consequences of our choices, and the three of these bear out those choices for eternity.

Heaven is being with God and all that this entails: Perfect love, joy and peace. No more pain, sorrow, rejection, anger – only perfection with Christ. It is the place where we become what we have been created to be: one with God. Heaven is the fire of God's presence. We are used to hell being described as a burning place, but, in actuality, the best description of heaven is that of fire. God IS love and God's presence is a burning, consuming fire.

As we draw closer to that fire, that which is not authentic – that which is not a part of what we were created to be – gets burned up, and that can be painful. Thus, we have purgatory.

Purgatory is God's severe mercy. Despite the fact that we may, while on earth, desire to be with God, we still make terrible mistakes. We sin, hurt others and neglect God and our faith. When we do this, we accumulate on our souls the consequences (the dirt) of sin. As we draw closer to God, those things need to burn up so that we can be the pure gold, without stain or defect. This process is called purgation – purgatory. We believe it can happen on earth and it definitely happens at our death. Once in purgatory, we are going to heaven, because while our "yes" to God may be imperfect, it is a "yes," and he'll take it!

Hell. Yikes! This begins on earth with the pain we feel when we neglect our relationship with God. It is the consequence of a life spent seeking our own way and the pleasures of the world as opposed to God's way. When we spend our lifetime ignoring or hating God, we have chosen to be separated from him. At our death, God respects that choice and does not make us live with him. Thus, we have hell. The pain in hell is not so much physical as it is spiritual. Our souls are made to be with God and in hell, we are separate. That's what makes hell so bad.

Whew! That was a lot of information. Be sure and check your *catechism* on these. There is so much more to say, especially in these sections: **heaven *(1729, 1821, 2796)*, hell *(1034 -1037)*, purgatory *(1030-1032)*.**

Warning! Bad joke ahead!

I heard a great story recently about two nuns traveling together in a car. As they rode along, they saw off in the distance the devil on a road sign making fun of them. They couldn't believe it! The first nun says, "What do I do?" The second nun said calmly, "Stay calm, Sister, and pray!" Thus, they began to pray. Next, the devil turned into a bat that was flying around the car. Again, the first nun says, "What do I do now?" The second nun said, "Stay calm, Sister, and pray." As she began her prayers, the bat stuck to their windshield! Shocked, the first sister said, "Sister, what do I do now?" The second nun responded, "Quick, show him your cross!" So the first nun rolled down the window and screamed, "Get off the windshield now, you stupid bat!"

Chapter Two: Questions about the church

Dear Fr. Joe,
What does the church teach about cremation? What happens to us when we die? Do we believe in reincarnation?

To the untrained observer, these questions may appear unrelated, but I, the answer man, shall mash them all together to create an answer stew. Brace yourself! The answer to all of these questions can be found in the idea of the value of the human body in the Catholic faith.

First of all, and perhaps most important, as Catholics, we believe in the resurrection of the body. That's right, we believe these bodies are going to heaven some day. Where does this come from? If you look in *Genesis*, you'll see that after God finished with creation, he said, "It is good." He was talking about us, as well as the rest of creation, and no amount of sin on our part can change something God declared good. Also, we Catholics believe that when Jesus took flesh, he made all flesh sacred. With all these things in mind, I like to tell people that if I lose weight, I will lose some of my sanctity, but nobody seems to believe me.

Anyway, with this understanding, we know now that we reject any theology that teaches that the body is just a shell or a container for our souls. We believe that this body is sacred and is in fact going to spend an eternity with Jesus. Incidentally, that is why we have so many rules about these bodies of ours.

Where do we get this theology? Well, we're Catholic, so we get it from two places. First of all, the Bible. We've already looked at *Genesis* and Jesus taking flesh, but there are other biblical references. In *I Corinthians 6:13-15, 19-20*, Paul lays down our belief in the resurrection of the body. Read this one; it's very important. Also in *I Corinthians 15:50-56* Paul describes how our "heavenly bodies" will be different (this does not mean perfect abs, I checked).

That covers some of the Sacred Scripture passages, so let's take a look at the *catechism*. Your *catechism, section 990*, states, "The resurrection of the flesh means not only that the immortal soul will live on after death, but that even our mortal body will come to life again." Also in *CCC, see sections 686, 999-1000*.

So, if our bodies are sacred and, in fact, destined for heaven, then we have the beginnings of the answers to our questions. Ready? First of all, the Catholic Church rejects the idea of reincarnation. If our bodies are destined for heaven, which one do we get at the resurrection? Our *catechism* says that there is no "pool of souls" for reincarnated beings. For the Scripture, please see *Hebrews 9:27*. Cremation is acceptable in the Catholic Church.

The **CCC** puts it this way: "The church permits cremation, provided that it does not demonstrate a denial of faith in the resurrection of the body." *(2301)*. It is important to note that the actual cremation is to be done after the funeral Mass.

What happens when we die? That one is a little more involved. Putting it in the briefest possible terms, we will face two judgments; first, the specific judgment at the moment of our death. This is the one you hear all the jokes about "standing before the gates of heaven." This judgment takes place at our deaths and our souls bear this decision out, but not our bodies (yet!). Secondly, at the end of time, when Jesus returns, all of creation will be judged and our souls will join our bodies at our final destination.

What about scattering ashes or wearing ashes in a piece of jewelry?

We need to avoid this. We must treat the deceased body as we would a non-cremated body. The ashes must be placed in a single container and buried in a columbarium or graveyard.

I know that some have taken the ashes of their beloved dead and placed them in amulets that they wear. Again, this is not the way we would treat the body of one who was not cremated, so we don't do it to one that is.

So, what if we have done one or more of these things already? Keep in mind a really simple premise: God does not judge us for what we do not know, through no fault of our own. All of us have made mistakes in unintentional ignorance. I truly can't imagine anyone treating the dead in a way the church tells us not to out of malice. So, as God asks us to do every day of our lives, we learn from our errors and accept God's wonderful, loving and freely given mercy.

Warning! Bad joke ahead!

True story: One day, as I walked toward the reconciliation chapel to hear confessions, a young boy came up to me. He was really excited about next year being his year to celebrate first reconciliation, and he wanted to practice his Act of Contrition on me. I smiled and said, "Sure, let's hear it." He took on a look of total concentration and began, flying through the prayer without one mistake. He got to the end and said, " ... I promise to sin no more and avoid ... " Then he paused, looked at me and said, "Is that right? Sin no more?" I smiled and nodded, so he said, "Then why do I have to memorize the prayer?"

Chapter Two: Questions about the church

Dear Fr. Joe,
Am I sinning if I am supposed to keep the Sabbath day holy, but I go to work?

It's like my dad used to say, "Son, some things are like a horse in a telephone booth – you just can't get around it." OK, Dad never said that ... but, if you can't get around it, then you can't. So, what do you do?

First of all, make sure that whatever work you do, whenever you do it, you do it for the Lord, conscious of the gifts he gave you to make it possible. Second, make sure you get to church each weekend, and dedicate one day to God in a special way – paying special attention to family and friends, spending some extra time in prayer and just plain relaxing. God doesn't demand the impossible of us. God asks that we follow him in the best way we can. Whenever we find ourselves in a situation where we aren't able to follow the letter of the law, then we should be sure that we follow the heart of it.

Dear Fr. Joe,
What is devotionalism? My priest said it is a bad thing, but some of my fellow parishioners disagree. What's the truth here?

An "ism" is a tricky concept. For some people, praying to saints is their definition of "devotionalism." And, for others, not praying 15 different kinds of devotions a day is negligence. So, where is the answer?

St. Thomas Aquinas would say that it is in the middle.

Devotions are a perfectly valid and powerful way for Catholics to express our faith in Jesus. However, like all good things, it sometimes gets taken to an extreme. It's like country music in that regard. I guess a couple songs a year on the radio can be acceptable, but entire radio stations dedicated to it? That is a sin of SOME kind, I'm sure.

Seriously, though, sometimes, there are people who take their devotions too far and neglect all other areas of spirituality and prayer. Folks may get to the point where they teach that if you don't pray their specific kinds of devotions, you are in jeopardy of hell. That is devotionalism and it is a bad thing.

However, completely neglecting devotions is bad also, right? We need the intercessions of the saints or God would not have offered them to us.

So, let's make sure we find the meeting place in the middle and pray as we should.

Dear Fr. Joe,
Why should I be confirmed? What does it mean to be an "active member of the church"?

In order for you to be an active member of the church, you have to be taught by example. This is where your parents come in: by word and example, does your mom and/or dad show that their faith is the most important thing? Do they understand that confirmation is not some sort of "Catholic rite of passage," but an empowerment with the Spirit that raised Jesus from the dead?

What this means is that you are coming into a time when your faith is no longer your parents' faith, but your own. This means that you take responsibility for getting yourself to church at least once a week and confession at least twice a year. This means that you allow the Holy Spirit to get inside you and work wonders in your life and the lives of those around you.

An active member of the church is someone who has surrendered to the gift of the Spirit and allowed Jesus into his or her heart. They show this by giving of their time and talents to the church. That is a basic idea of what it means to be an active member of the church.

Remember, our faith is not private. As Catholics, we embrace our faith in a community of believers. We can't blow off church with the excuse that "I follow God in my own way." That is a cop out.

Think of this: when we go to church, we find ourselves surrounded by saints and sinners, all of whom we are called to love. It is too easy to say that we love God and never have to challenge ourselves to love God's people. When we do it alone, we run the risk of never having our ability to love challenged. We avoid contemplating God's divine presence in the people we don't like or are even afraid of.

To you and your parents, it is my firm opinion that if you don't wish to be confirmed, you shouldn't be. This is NOT something you "get done" or "get out of the way." The Spirit is too great of a gift to be used like that.

I am going to answer your question in a roundabout way, but it all goes back to one word: commitment.

This morning, my alarm went off at 5 a.m. Like every day, I rolled over, turned the alarm off, grabbed a good, stinky, nasty cup of coffee and started slugging it down. (My motto on coffee: If it doesn't make my eyes bleed, it's not strong enough.) Then I took a shower and sat down to pray. At that moment, whether I felt like it or not, I was a priest.

Then I went down to my office to look at my day. I dedicated it to God and promised him I would work hard at being a good priest. I knew that no matter what I had to do, whether I felt like doing it or not, today, I was a priest. I met with some people, got called to the hospital, sat through meetings, and took Communion to someone who was very ill at home. Through it all, I was a priest − whether I felt like it or not.

So there it is: COMMITMENT! I know from watching my parents who have been married 41 years that it is all about commitment. The joy of marriage is not found in maintaining a feeling of love, but in living out a commitment to be who and where God calls us to be − whether we feel like it or not. Priests know a lot about commitment. Their wisdom can be of help.

Dear Fr. Joe,
My daughter is bringing her boyfriend home for the holidays and insists on sleeping in the same room with him. I'm opposed to that. What should I do?

Insists? It's your house. She should insist on nothing but respect for your household and the rules you have.

You are right to be opposed to what your daughter wants. Too many people fall easily into serious sexual sins with no thought of the spiritual or physical consequences of their actions. By forbidding her from sleeping with her boyfriend in your house, you are protecting her dignity, your house and the sacrament of marriage. If they want to live as married people, they should get married.

I know, I know! You are thinking, "Yeah, Father, I figured that part out. But how do I handle the conflict?"

I would have to say that, in this situation, conflict is unavoidable. So, what are the rules here? Above and beyond what will be written in this magazine, I believe that the key is to hold fast to what you know to be true.

You can sit her down and gently explain to her why what she is doing is wrong and that you can't support it. You don't do this for any other reason than love for her. I know this can feel like you are being too harsh or even unloving. However, I assure you that as long as you do this in love, you are doing what is right.

Dear Fr. Joe,
Why should I go to a priest to talk about marriage when a priest doesn't have any experience in marriage?

Not too long ago, I was reading an article in the paper. In it, a married man wrote an article about the priesthood. He had several thoughts about what priests should be, and he challenged the celibacy of priesthood. At one point, he asked, "How can a celibate man tell my wife and me anything about marriage?" Am I the only one catching the irony here?

I learned much about my priesthood in the seminary. I have also learned about my priesthood from the thoughts, ideas and support of the larger Catholic community including married couples, single folks, and other religious.

The reality is, we all have gifts of wisdom from two sources: experience and observation. Which one can a priest offer? Both. You see, despite the fervent expressions of denial on my parents' part, I was raised in a home with a mother and father, some sisters and brothers, etc. I saw and experienced many elements of married and family life. Also, in the seminary I was taught many ideas on how to help couples that have proven effective in my time at parishes. From observation and experience, I have some idea of what works and what doesn't. And I am happy to share that with couples who ask.

Warning! Bad joke ahead!

A couple was having some trouble so they came to see me in my office. After some time, I felt that I had discovered the root of the problem. I stood up, went over to the woman, asked her to stand, and gave her a hug. I looked at the husband and said, "This is what your wife needs at least once a day!" The man frowned, thought for a moment and then said, "OK, what time do you want me to bring her back tomorrow?"

Chapter Two: Questions about the church

Dear Fr. Joe,
Why does the church require nine months of preparation before marriage? If couples feel they are ready, why is the church making them wait?

Great question! Let's take a look at a couple of ideas that will help in answering your question.

First of all, like priesthood, marriage is a vocation. Training for a priestly vocation is an eight-to-10-year process. We study the meaning of the priesthood; we practice different elements of the priesthood; and, we take time for prayer and discernment so that we can keep ourselves centered in Jesus Christ and his church as good spiritual leaders. It's a long and difficult process that helped me tremendously, despite all evidence to the contrary.

When we look at the state of marriage in our country, can we honestly say more preparation isn't necessary? We give hours of our day, days of our week, weeks of our month and years to television and the ideas about marriage that are presented to us there. We have been so "catechized" by the TV that nine months of exposure to Catholic catechesis seem nowhere near enough.

You see, getting married in the Catholic Church is not to be done lightly. The church has a vision for marriage and family. By marrying in the church we are saying we want to be a part of that vision. So, in the nine months of preparation, engaged couples learn about that vision – the vocational aspect of marriage. It is in this preparation that we ensure the couple agrees with that vision (at least in principle) and are willing to live it as best they can with the help of God. Again, much the same as I did in my preparation for priesthood.

One of the best examples of this vision is the church's teaching on the life-giving aspect of marriage. Most couples I have met with do not understand why the church has such a "problem" with artificial birth control. They have heard of Natural Family Planning (NFP) only through critical and mocking references in the media. Marriage preparation allows the couple a chance to be exposed to the beauty of the church's teaching. The testimony of many couples who practice NFP was enough to convince me that it can be an incredible, life-changing experience. If a couple is hustled through marriage preparation, they may miss this amazing teaching.

And, frankly, a couple who feel they are ready for marriage may be wrong. How many times in your own life have you been sure you were right about something, only to discover you were not? Now, that never happens to me, but I have heard about it from people who come to talk to me. A marriage preparation program may help a couple determine whether they are ready or not.

By immersing themselves in the wisdom of the church, engaged couples will find they are better prepared for marriage psychologically, spiritually and emotionally. Couples want their marriages to succeed, right? Why not enter into it as strong as possible?

Once a couple is married, please remember the church. We are here for you – please come to us when you need help. We all get by with a little help from our friends.

Warning! Bad joke ahead!

I was talking to a parishioner who shared a great insight. She was speaking about her kids and how much she loved them. But, like any other kind of love, it is challenged sometimes by her kids' ... hmmm ... shall we say "intense energy levels?" Anyway, she has gotten into the habit of looking in on them after they fall asleep because they "look so angelic." Then, one night, this realization hit her: They aren't just sleeping – they're recharging!

Dear Fr. Joe,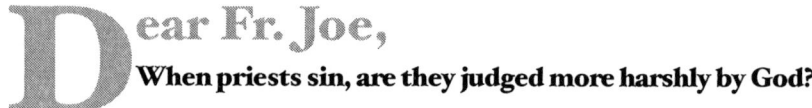
When priests sin, are they judged more harshly by God?

Yes and no. How is that for a safe answer? But it is true, so let's look at how:

The answer is no because of the nature of sin. To put it in a really complicated way: sin is sin. A lay person committing a sin and a priest committing a sin have affected their souls in the same way. In both situations, the soul is separated from God, and you can't put a price tag on how painful that is.

Having said that, I will now contradict myself. Yes, a priest is judged more harshly by God. This is not because of the nature of sin; it is because of the nature of the priesthood. If a person in the grocery store shares his or her opinion on a spiritual matter and is wrong, the effects are not nearly as large as a priest giving a homily based on bad theology before 1,200 people in church. Just ask the people who've had to suffer through some of my homilies!

Also, it is worse because of the potential scandal that is involved. As we know, reported sins by priests have caused tremendous pain, embarrassment and suspicion among Catholics everywhere. Obviously, the sins of a few priests have brought suffering to all Catholics – priest and laity alike – and because of the greater impact of these sins, the judgment for them, if not repented, is expected to be harsher.

For example, a priest in the confessional can turn someone off to the sacrament of reconciliation for the rest of their lives. A priest having a bad day and saying something hurtful can be someone's excuse for not going to church for the rest of their lives.

Dear Fr. Joe,
The priest who baptized my children left the priesthood under some very bad circumstances. Should I have my children re-baptized?

This answer may surprise you but, according to the Catholic Church, there is no such thing as "re-baptism!" It's like the Detroit Lions and a winning record – it can't happen. Let's take a look at why.

A long time ago, there was a heresy called Donatism (pronounced just like it looks) where it was said the power of a sacrament depended on the sanctity of the priest who administered it. St. Augustine said that was not possible because it would make the sinfulness of a priest stronger than the power of God. And that just can't be!

As priests, we are vessels of God's power. Some days we are better vessels than others, but our sinfulness does not have the power to overcome God. Through the authority and power of Jesus, the church appointed us to administer the sacraments.

I can easily and honestly say I have had some bad days and said or did things that hurt people. When I have a day like that, I hope others will show me the mercy that Jesus has shown all of us and forgive me and allow me to be what I am: a fallen human desperately in need of God's grace and help. To me, this makes a priest a better leader or spiritual helper. I know how badly I need God and I am able to share that need with others.

Warning! Bad joke ahead!

I have never been on a cruise, but one of my friends has. He told me a great story about his experience. He said that as they sailed the seas and were looking at the sunset, everyone on the boat could see a bearded man on a small island, jumping up and down, waving his arms in the air and shouting. My buddy said he turned to the captain and said, "I wonder who that is." The captain said, "I have no idea. But every year when we pass that island, he goes crazy."

Dear Fr. Joe,
If I am saved through my baptism, then why do I need to go to a priest for confession?

Well, that's a good question, but there a few issues that need to be addressed.

Are we saved through baptism? The answer, interestingly enough, is yes and no. Baptism offers us salvation, but it demands a response from us. Through baptism, God reaches out to us and offers us his unconditional and perfect love.

Now, such an intense act of love on the part of God demands a response from us. The ritual of baptism itself demands a response from us. For us to receive baptism and not respond through communal and private prayer, and a life of loving God and neighbor, is to condemn ourselves. A part of this response is continually reconciling with God and the world around us.

So, why go to a priest? Take for example the following hypothetical situation:

Now, let's say there is a priest who writes a question and answer column for a magazine. Suppose said priest is given questions months in advance and is asked to turn in his column on a specific date. Say it is now two months after that specified deadline and three or four threatening phone calls have been received by said priest/columnist from his magazine editor. So, under severe strain from the need to get that particular month's issue out, the editor goes into a rage and hits the priest over the head with a baseball bat, rendering him unconscious and out of commission for two weeks.

Later, being a person of good conscience, the editor goes to the priest in the hospital and asks his forgiveness. Because this priest is a man of great kindness and compassion, slow to anger, quick to forgive and abounding in generosity, he forgives the editor. Now, for the million dollar question: Does the priest's head still hurt?

Of course it does!

Not only that, but people who counted on that priest during the two weeks he was out of commission are STILL without a priest.

Basically, this sin – like all other sin – is like the old telephone company ad: It reaches out and touches someone – in fact, lots of people. All of our sins work that way. Each sin affects us in ways that we never think about and hurts people we may never even have met!

What do we need to do? We need someone to stand in the place of all those affected by our sin and forgive us for the consequences we will never know. To offend someone and ask for God's forgiveness is being naive as to the nature of the sin. Thus, one reason we go to a priest for forgiveness is because he stands in *persona ecclesia* – in the person of the church – and forgives us on behalf of all those affected by our sins.

The other issue concerning your question is found in Scripture and tradition. In the ***Gospel of John*** it says,

> *Jesus breathed on them and said to them, "Receive the Holy Spirit. Whose sins you forgive are forgiven them, and whose sins you retain are retained." (Jn 20:22-23)*

Jesus gave the disciples that specific power of forgiveness which the disciples then passed onto their successors. It has been passed on from generation to generation. A 2,000-year-old unbroken chain carries those words of Jesus to our present day. This system of sacramental confession was given to us by none other than Jesus.

Dear Fr. Joe,
What is the problem with general absolution – going to confession in a large group?

Before I answer this question, let's take a look at what general absolution is. When we celebrate the sacrament of reconciliation, there are three ways to do it. The first way is the one with which we are most familiar. It is when we go to a priest and confess individually. This is rite one.

The second way we can celebrate the sacrament of reconciliation is within the context of a reconciliation or penance service. Here, the church recognizes the impact of sin on both the individual and community. After a Celebration of the Word, individual confession and absolution takes place. This is the way we celebrate reconciliation when we go to penance services during Lent and Advent. This is rite two.

General absolution is when the priest is so outnumbered there is no hope of hearing the confessions of all of those present. Specifically, this would be in a situation where a large number of people are going into combat, or some other situation where lives are at risk. In this situation, the priest will take the group through an examination of conscience and then do one prayer of absolution for everyone present. This is rite three.

So, technically, there is no "problem" with general absolution. The problem is when it is used inappropriately – when general absolution becomes the norm instead of the exception.

Smart answers & bad jokes

Dear Fr. Joe,

In churches, why did they remove the tabernacle from the main sanctuary and place it off to the side? Why are we hiding Jesus away?

First of all, there are two appropriate places for the tabernacle in the church. It can be in the sanctuary or in a separate chapel. The United States bishops released an important document about the design and structure of churches – ***Built of Living Stones***. In paragraph *#74* we read, "The bishop is to determine where the tabernacle will be placed and to give further direction. The bishop may decide that the tabernacle is to be placed in the sanctuary apart from the altar of celebration or in a separate chapel suitable for adoration and the private prayer of the faithful." Our bishop allows either. Let's take a look at both.

One option is to place the tabernacle in the sanctuary of the church. There are definite bonuses to this approach. With the tabernacle in plain sight, it is another reminder that we are a eucharistic people. If the tabernacle is to be located in the sanctuary, it should be placed so that it "does not draw the attention of the faithful away from the eucharistic celebration." *(#79)* It also should allow for those periods of quiet prayer outside the celebration of the Eucharist. *(ibid.)* Since the altar itself is a symbol of Christ and the place where we offer our eucharistic sacrifice, the bishops suggest that consideration be given to using lighting, distance or some other architectural device to separate the tabernacle and reservation area during Mass. *(#80)*

The other option is to designate a separate chapel for the tabernacle, which is "connected to the church and conspicuous to the faithful. The placement and design of the chapel can foster reverence and can provide the quiet and focus needed for personal prayer, and it should provide kneelers and chairs for those who come to pray." *(#77)* This, too, has distinct bonuses. With a separate chapel, prayer and adoration are possible in a special room affording more privacy. With a chapel for the Blessed Sacrament, we are making a powerful statement: This place is special. A separate chapel can also be a physical sign of the importance of the Eucharist.

In general, the church provides norms that express the importance of the Blessed Sacrament and the tabernacle that houses it. There should be only one tabernacle in a church; it should be beautifully designed, and in harmony with the decor of the rest of the church. *(#72)*

So where are we then? Hopefully, we are in a place where we can all agree that the Eucharist must be honored. Some churches will choose to honor the Blessed Sacrament in the sanctuary itself; others will honor it with a chapel. Both ways work.

The bishop and his Office of Worship help a parish determine which is best for them and their worship space.

The Eucharist is who we are. Its centrality in our liturgical life and our prayer life is, in many ways, what distinguishes us as Catholic Christians. We believe that in the Eucharist, Jesus offers himself to us in a real and physical way. Let's take today and thank God for the great gift of the Eucharist and dedicate our lives to him.

If moving the tabernacle to a side chapel causes you pain, consider praying about it before the Blessed Sacrament – wherever it is.

Dear Fr. Joe,

There are a lot of different religions out there and everybody thinks theirs is right. One of my friends says that we are all right. Is it true that all religions are right?

Nope. One of the things about our culture that is beautiful is our intense desire to be accepting people. When we do this, we can be acting in a way that is very Christ-like. However, sometimes in our efforts to be open people, we sometimes accept too much. Or, as one of my classmates at seminary put it, "You can be so open-minded that your brain falls out."

Jesus came as a divine person who was many things: the Son of God, our Hope, our Savior, all these and more. But Jesus also came as the truth. Check out the ***catechism, section 2466***: "In Jesus Christ, the whole of God's truth has been made manifest. 'Full of grace and truth,' He came as the 'light of the world,' He is the Truth." Wow! How is that for powerful!

As we worship Jesus, we believe we are worshiping the truth. Some people will tell you that truth is subjective. They say, "You have your truth and I have mine." That, my brothers and sisters, is just plain wrong. There is only one truth and we can participate in it fully or partially.

There always is and always will be things that are more truthful than others and this includes our relationship with God.

Now, let's look at how the statement, "You have your truth and I have mine," doesn't hold water in Christianity, or even the practical world. What if I were to say that your car is red while you say it is maize and blue. Now, as beautiful as those two colors are when put together on say, a football helmet, it's not like your car would appear maize and blue to me and red to you, right?

Since we now know that there is truth out there and it is not subjective, or a matter of opinion, then we have an obligation as humans to find out what the truth is.

Warning! Bad joke ahead!

I was chatting with an absent-minded gentleman during Communion calls. He told me about this great new restaurant that he said I "had to try." I asked him for the name of the place and he paused. "Can't remember," he mumbled. "Son, what do ya call that thing with a bud on the end of it? It's got thorns and you give it to people you love?" "A Rose?" I ventured. "That's it!" he exclaimed. Then, he turned to his wife. "ROSE! What's the name of that restaurant we went to the other night?"

Dear Fr. Joe,
What are the holy days of obligation and what does it mean when we have one?

OK, let's start right off with a list of the days that the U.S. Conference of Catholic Bishops has decreed are holy days of obligation:

- Jan. 1 – the solemnity of Mary, Mother of God
- Seventh Sunday of Easter – the solemnity of the Ascension
- Aug. 15 – the solemnity of the Assumption of the Virgin Mary
- Nov. 1 – the solemnity of All Saints
- Dec. 8 – the solemnity of the Immaculate Conception
- Dec. 25 – the solemnity of the Nativity of Our Lord Jesus Christ

Whenever Jan. 1, the solemnity of Mary, Mother of God, or Aug. 15, the solemnity of the Assumption, or Nov. 1, the solemnity of All Saints, falls on a Saturday or on a Monday, the obligation to attend Mass is removed.

So, what does this mean? That on the days listed above, Catholics everywhere, who are able, are obligated by their baptism to go to church and celebrate Mass.

What does "who are able" mean? It means those who are physically able to attend and have the resources to get to Mass. We should never miss these days because of sporting events or a busy social calendar.

If we are sick, we are not obligated. Be sure and check with your local pastor on what his expectations are.

Now, if you want a great link to look up how the U.S. bishops break it down, go to *www.usccb.org/liturgy/q%26a/general/obligation.shtml* and poke around. There is some great information there.

Warning! Bad joke ahead!

While on vacation, I stopped to fill my tank, but apparently, everybody else did, too. When I finally got to a pump after a significant wait, the guy at the pump next to me said, "Crazy, isn't it, Father? It seems as if everyone waits until the last minute to get ready for a long trip." I laughed and said, "I know. It's the same in my line of work."

Dear Fr. Joe,

What gives the church the authority to determine what is right and wrong? As far as I know, there is nothing on birth control, capital punishment, genetic engineering and/or cloning in the Bible. Doesn't it just hurt the credibility of the church when it is wrong (i.e., Galileo)?

What a packed question! What we have here is a super-relevant question with a lot of layers, so let's get right to it.

First, let's start by making sure we are on common ground. I am learning that there are, basically, two groups of people who ask questions such as these. The first group desires to learn God's ways so that they can follow them. The second group asks the question to collect "God's opinion." They then decide if they agree or disagree with it.

My presumption is that you are in the first group. You, like holy people for thousands of years, say in the words of King David, "Teach me, Lord, your way that I may walk in your truth." *(Ps 86:11)* We seek what God teaches so that we can follow it. This is the call of Catholics everywhere and at all times. So, how do we seek those ways?

As you know, Scripture gives us clear explanation of many moral issues. For example, adultery, murder, stealing, etc. are wrong. Caring for the lowest members of society and obeying God are essential. God loves us passionately and intensely. All these things (and more) are clear.

Scripture also gives us a clear understanding of God: who he is, his love for us, and his desire that we have abundant life, and a future full of hope.

However, seeing as though modern moral issues are, well, modern, they are not mentioned in Scripture. To tackle this problem, we look at the issues that are mentioned in Scripture, and we look at who God is, and what he desires for humanity. When we do this, a clear, consistent vision of life emerges that points us toward the answers to questions not yet asked when Scripture was written. This process is the beginning of sacred tradition.

So, who articulates sacred tradition? What gives these "know-it-all theologians and bishops" the right to tell us what to do? Now, technically it's not "what" gives the church authority to determine right and wrong; it's "who." As Catholics, we believe that Jesus gave the apostles authority to interpret Sacred Scripture and tradition and guide us in our walk with Christ. Therefore, who gives them the right? Ultimately, I, you and anyone who accepts that the church was established by Jesus Christ when he gave Peter the keys to the kingdom.

In the end, I hope we take the teachings of Sacred Scripture and sacred tradition and write them into our hearts and become people of life. I hope we see and live the words of Scripture that our bodies are temples of the Holy Spirit (by the way, when I got dressed this morning, I noticed I seem to be adding on to my temple). I pray that we see that everyone we meet is someone for whom God laid down his life. I hope we learn that the experience of life is so sacred and blessed that we want to make sure that the dignity and value of the human person is articulated and defended in all our decisions.

I find it excellent that you brought up our past mistakes (Galileo). We need to remember these mistakes, so that we can see that these flawed vessels of God still are capable of offering us a perfect vision. Despite our past sins, the magisterium (teaching authority of the church) has never erred in declarations of faith and doctrine. As Dr. Cooney at Sacred Heart Seminary put it "God writes straight with crooked lines." I love that line. It reminds me that perfect performance is not a prerequisite for serving God.

We remember our past, not so that we can be paralyzed by guilt, but so that we can be free to accept God's gratuitous, unearned love with pure hearts. Have we made mistakes in the past? Oh yes; we've made some doozies! Will we make more in the future? I would assume so. Will God still guide, protect and love us? Absolutely. Blessed be the name of God. Enjoy another day in God's presence!

"For God, love and life are so interlinked as to be indistinguishable. Where God gives His love, God gives His life. Where God gives His life, God gives His love." – Alice von Hildebrand.

Chapter Two: Questions about the church

Dear Fr. Joe,
What's so great about the priesthood? Why did you decide to become a priest?

On and off through my life, I felt a call to the priesthood. Sometimes I nurtured it; other times, I buried it. The idea scared me, to be sure, but I have to say that the desire never went away. There were, in retrospect, four key events that eventually brought me to the seminary in August 1993.

First, I had two long talks with a priest, Father John Bertalucci. He spoke with me and prayed with me, helping me to see not only what God wanted, but helping me find the strength to do it.

Second, at a conference in Pittsburgh, a bishop, Sam Jacobs, from Louisiana sat down and spoke to me in a way I have never forgotten.

Third, my family and friends supported me as best they could: prayed with me, encouraged me, challenged me, etc. This helped me not only to see what God wanted, but also to have the courage to follow through with it.

Finally, people were patient with me and forgiving. Feeling called to the priesthood can be a confusing thing, and I had difficulty locating a priest who was willing and able to help me. I found myself unable to express what I was feeling to anyone I thought would understand. As a result, I found myself frustrated and made some mistakes along the way and hurt people. People were (and are!) very merciful and supportive. What a great thing that is.

Once in the seminary, the teachers and staff were amazing. They showed me how to love the church and serve her as a priest. I met other young men (and some not so young!) who wanted to be priests also. Sacred Heart Seminary was one of God's greatest gifts to me and I am proud to have gone there and learned all that I did.

Warning! Bad joke ahead!

I had a buddy coming to see me the other day. On the radio, I heard an update that there was a car driving in the wrong direction on the highway. Realizing my friend was probably on that highway in the area of the problem, I called his cell and told him he needed to be careful because a car was heading in the wrong direction near him. He laughed and said, "It's not just one car, man. They're all going the wrong way but me!" Ah, the wonders of pride.

Dear Fr. Joe,

Why is pride a sin – what about pride in your work or family? Is there a good kind of pride? If so, what kind of pride is sinful?

Great question! I am glad someone finally asked me about pride because, frankly, I am the master of humility. I am the most humble man I know; a virtual standard for humility. So much so that I am currently working on a book called *Humility and How It Made Me Great*. I am sure it will be a best-seller. Then, I will write a sequel called *The Three Most Humble People in the World* and *How I Trained the Other Two*. I could keep going you know ...

Back to the question, the glossary of the **catechism** describes pride as "One of the seven capital sins. Pride is undue self-esteem or self-love, which seeks attention and honor and sets oneself in competition with God." Let's break that down.

In order to grow in holiness, we need to grow in self-knowledge. Pope John Paul II wrote about this in his book, *The Acting Person,* and he spoke about it in numerous addresses. Self-knowledge is when we have a realistic view of ourselves and an idea of what our weaknesses and strengths are. We need both of these things to have a healthy concept of ourselves. Now, the opposite of that healthy self-knowledge is found in pride.

So, to figure out what is good and what is sinful, let's look at some specific examples and see what we learn.

OK, first, let's say that we are good at something. If we are good at something, and we are aware that we are good at it, it is not prideful to acknowledge that fact. That is speaking the truth. St. Francis of Assisi is quoted as saying, "True humility begins with our ability to recognize our weaknesses as well as our strengths."

On the other hand, if we know we are good at something and then say we aren't good at it, we'd be lying. This is called false humility. This is when we refuse compliments and deny our goodness at certain things. We may even claim that God cannot love us and that "sets oneself in competition with God."

If it is hard for you to take compliments, then try this: the next time people compliment you, let's consider it a prayer. That person making the compliment is thanking God through you for the gift you manifest.

That does bring up an important point. I think one of the reasons that we all have trouble accepting compliments is that we don't have any practice. Think about how hard it is for us to compliment and receive compliments.

I firmly believe that one of the greatest weaknesses among the Catholic family is that we are so very specific with our criticisms and so very general with our praise. I challenge myself and everyone reading this column today to dedicate ourselves to studying people, looking at their lives and seeing where they are strong. We do the opposite naturally and easily – ever notice that? When we then see someone's gifts, we must take that truth to them and honor them for it. Think of how far a very generous compliment will take you and then share that joy with someone else.

Believe it or not, this will help us all be more humble.

With all this in mind, I hope we see that it is a good thing to take pride in our work if we are good workers. It is a good thing to take pride in our family if we love and honor them and are encouraging them to be faithful to the mission of Jesus and the church.

I think that in the end, the key to a healthy balance between too much pride and false humility is to recognize where our gifts came from and be grateful to God for giving them to us. Another key is to make sure and observe our brothers' and sisters' strengths and share them in a specific way. The final point is to then take the strengths we see in ourselves or that others have seen in us and dedicate them to working for Jesus and his bride, the church.

Dear Fr. Joe,

Some people say God will bless you with money if you live right. They also say it's the devil's fault if you live in poverty. Is this true?

This question will really help us to see some key ideas in our faith.

Now, there are times when living in poverty is the fault of the devil. For example, if we are wasteful with our money and spend it on things we don't need, then it is because of our sin that we live in poverty. Or, if we spend our money on things like drugs, alcohol and Michigan State University apparel, then yes, our poverty is our own fault and we need to get help.

Sometimes, evil is the root cause of poverty, but it is not evil-doing on the part of the person living in poverty. Greed, abuse and mismanagement in our health-care systems have put many good and innocent people in a position where medical problems can lead to financial ruin. We also know that many of the super-wealthy running our nation's big corporations have destroyed the lives of innocent men and women through their greed. Make no mistake, these men and women who lie on financial reports to add zeroes to an already healthy income are doing the devil's work. And poverty resulting from their actions is the work of the devil.

If you have been a victim of any of these, or similar, situations or circumstances, then your poverty is a result of man's cooperation with the devil, but not YOUR cooperation. However, the idea that poverty is always a sign of sin in the poor person is faulty to its core. If that were true, then Jesus was in trouble. Jesus not only lived as a traveling itinerant preacher; he spoke of how God identifies with the poor. He told a wealthy would-be follower that "foxes have holes and birds have nests, but the Son of Man has no place to lay his head." *(Mt 8:20)* Jesus lived right, no doubt, so I think we can dispel the issue of poverty being related to right behavior as a matter of principle.

But all that I have stated so far relates to the causes of poverty and provides little or no help. If you are not living in poverty, then the rest of this article is for you. This part of my column is a challenge and a wake-up call to all readers who can help the poor. We must give our time, resources, love and prayers. We can sacrifice and not buy things we do not need and, instead, give that money to those who don't have the basics. We can support candidates for political office who will fight evil in society, instead of promoting it. We can be involved politically in support of those who have no voice.

This year, please pray and challenge yourself to make a difference in the lives of people who suffer. It is nothing less than the call of the Gospel.

Warning! Bad joke ahead!

So, after Mass a few weeks ago, I was shaking hands and greeting people in the back of church when a little boy came up, hugged me and gave me a quarter.

"Well," I exclaimed, "what is this?"

He said, "It's all I've got, Father, but it's for you."

"Thank you," I replied, "but I'm OK. I don't need any money."

He looked at me and said, "I thought you'd need it. Dad says you are the poorest preacher he's ever heard of."

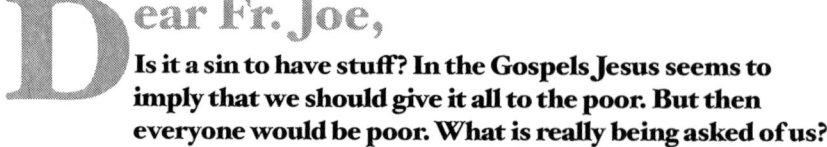

Dear Fr. Joe,

Is it a sin to have stuff? In the Gospels Jesus seems to imply that we should give it all to the poor. But then everyone would be poor. What is really being asked of us?

Jesus is asking us something that is very easy to express and very difficult to do – allow nothing to own us.

Chapter Two: Questions about the church

See, owning possessions is a good thing, but having the possessions own us is not. So, how do we tell the difference?

First of all, if we own something we can part with it at a moment's notice. Unless it is a necessity, we need to avoid being attached to anything we don't need.

I must say that I have been on the receiving end of some astounding generosity in the last year, and it has compelled me to be more generous in my own life. I have been challenged by others to sacrifice for others. I am trying to live the simple idea that giving out of my surplus is nice but giving out of my need is vital.

I feel freer than I ever have before. Go figure, Jesus was right.

I think it goes back to a fundamental attitude that Jesus challenges us to embrace. You and I are to see the world around us as our family. When I say this, there is the danger of us making it a "wouldn't it be nice" statement, but it is so much more than that. Jesus has made it so. You and I are connected by the body of Christ in an irrevocable way to the people of the world. That starving child in Bosnia – that's your son. The child dying of AIDS in Africa – your daughter. All of us are connected in the very body of Christ, and their pain is our pain. We must stop hoarding for ourselves and begin to sacrifice for the good of our biological family and our spiritual family.

Not too long ago, a friend and I were watching TV. The program we were watching was touring the homes of various movie stars. They got to the home of a very "socially conscious" movie star and the tour was astounding. In this gargantuan home, two massive rooms were built and designed for gift wrapping. Trust me, you read that right. Two huge rooms were set aside for the exclusive purpose of wrapping presents. When we saw this, my friend turned to me and said, "No kidding, Joe, that guy is going to have to stand in front of God and answer for that." He was right. Absolutely 100 percent right. We took it to the next step and challenged ourselves. What do I have that I don't need? Would I be willing to part with it to make someone's life better?

You may be reading this and thinking my approach is too radical. I suggest to you that our approach is not radical enough. It is quite possible we can be so busy taking care of ourselves and our immediate loved ones that we forget there is a world out there in need. We must draw ourselves out of our narrow view of the world and be challenged to work hard to make other people's lives livable.

So, how do we do it? I guess today would be a good day for all of us to go through our stuff and see what we can part with. That shirt you wear once a year would probably keep someone warmer this winter – the St. Vincent de Paul Society (and others) can make it happen. That money you were saving up to buy something you may not need can go to someone who doesn't have food, courtesy of the people at your local food bank. You get the idea, right? Please understand that Jesus demands this of us because he knows the truth – this mentality will set us free. We were created to live for others – and living for others will make us whole.

I had another idea about how we can take Jesus' teaching to the next level. I believe one of our most valuable tools in this society is our time. Look how we associate time with money – "saving time," "investing time," "time well spent" and of course, the obvious one, "time is money." So, let's start investing our time. Volunteer at your local Catholic school. Volunteer for St. Vincent de Paul or a local shelter. Help out a brother or sister by giving your most valuable assets – your time and energy. I hope this challenge starts us all on the path to Jesus.

Dear Fr. Joe,

I am troubled by a recent discovery. I saw in the news that a burial box (called an ossuary) was found that says Jesus had a brother. Is this true?

Let's go through what we know and what we don't know. Oh, and here is my disclaimer: I am not an expert!

What do we know? We know that in Silwan, on the West Bank right outside of Jerusalem, a limestone ossuary was found that contained an inscription in Aramaic. An anonymous Israeli collector purchased it in 1987 from an anonymous Palestinian in Israel. Dated to the first century, the ossuary has one line on it stating: "Ya'akov bar Yosef ahwi Yeshua," which means: "James, son of Joseph, brother of Jesus."

So, what is the big deal? For Catholics, the big deal seems to be the line "brother of Jesus." Some are using this to challenge the perpetual virginity of Mary – claiming she did not remain a virgin after the birth of Jesus and death of Joseph.

What should Catholics think? First of all, we should never be afraid of knowledge or science. As Catholics, we must always embrace learning more. If we truly believe what we say we believe, then we know that any discoveries made will only back us up, right?

Let's learn everything we can about this. My limited time only allows me so much research on the topic and I haven't found a solid Catholic response yet. In the meantime, what I have found suggests that the word "brother" may not have meant in Jesus' time and culture what it does now for us. "Brother," in this context, implies "cousin." Some have also said that Joseph could have been married before he married the Blessed Mother.

Either way, let's keep our eyes and ears open so we can learn all we can. In the future, I hope to talk about our belief in Mary's perpetual virginity and why that is important.

Dear Fr. Joe,
Why does the church seem so judgmental?

I appreciate how you worded your question – you avoided judging, didn't you? Way to go! Alright, on to the answer ...

I think many times, the church seems harsh and judgmental because she is trying to teach us difficult things. All of us have had that experience of having to be told the difficult thing. Usually, what helps us understand that the person is trying to help us is that we know them.

For example, I remember the time my mother told me to stop playing under power lines during thunderstorms. Sure, at first I was mad at her for cutting into my happy play time, but, in the end, I began to see that it was affecting me negatively. Hey, I was only 24.

OK, bad example. In the end, I guess what it comes down to is, when people we know have to tell us "the hard thing," it's easier to take than when a stranger does. Even if we disagree in the end, if we know them and know they love us, it's easier to take. Well, I think it can be hard to "know the church." And that can make the church seem harsh and judgmental sometimes.

So what do we do? I think we need to see that the motivation for the church is the same as it is for our parents or friends, who say the hard thing because they love us.

Looking at the word "respect," we see two Latin words brought together: *Re,* which means "again" and "*spect*" from a Latin root word meaning "to look at" – spectator, spectacles, etc. So, if we want to respect the church, we need to look at it again and see what it really is – our Christian Mother, teaching us right and wrong and guiding us in our lives.

Warning! Bad joke ahead!

I have a friend who runs a business where they reupholster furniture. Recently, he got sick, but, thank God he is fully recovered.

OK, that one was bad, I know. How about the one about the chicken who crossed the road? It was poultry in motion.

Dear Fr. Joe,

Is organ donation OK for Catholics? If yes, why? Doesn't the Bible say that our bodies rise from the dead? What about dividing up a potential saint for relics?

Great bunch of questions! In order to answer them, I am going to give us all some preliminary information that should, hopefully, clarify the church's teachings. In Scripture, we learn that we will experience two resurrections. First, our souls rise after we die. Second, our bodies join our souls at the second coming of Christ.

So, until the second coming, our souls are at their final judgment. Then, after Christ returns, our bodies rise to join our souls. This is just one of the reasons the church has so many teachings that revolve around respecting our bodies. Our bodies are destined for great things in the kingdom of God!

Anyway, with that background, let's see what the *catechism* has to say concerning organ donation:

Organ donation after death is a noble and meritorious act and is to be encouraged as an expression of generous solidarity. It is not morally acceptable if the donor or his proxy has not given explicit consent. Moreover, it is not morally admissible to bring about the disabling mutilation or death of a human being, even in order to delay the deaths of other persons. (ccc 2296)

For the relics question, the first place to look is the Bible: There are a few references to God granting miracles through the relics of holy people. *(cf II Kgs 13:10-21; Acts 19:11-12)* In ***II Kings***, we hear about the bones of Elisha bringing a dead man to life and in ***Acts***, a touch of Paul's handkerchiefs healed the sick and drove out demons.

With that history, early Christians were quite fond of relics from the saints being held up to veneration. How did they justify what appeared to be the mutilation of a corpse?

In the same way that the church accepts organ donations to save lives, the bones of saints have many potential benefits for us – they link us to the church of all ages and the veneration of relics has the potential to draw us closer to Christ. Because of these benefits, and with a strong belief in the resurrection of the body, the church does allow us to "divide up" our beloved saints to help us grow in holiness.

I will close with a quote from St. Jerome:

> *We do not worship, we do not adore, for fear that we should bow down to the creature rather than to the Creator, but we venerate the relics of the martyrs in order the better to adore him whose martyrs they are.* (**St. Jerome, Letter to Riparius**)

Warning! Bad joke ahead!

I had a mom tell me a story about her son. He missed Palm Sunday Mass because he was sick with the flu. She and the rest of her family returned home with their palm branches after church and checked on the boy. "What's the branch for, Mom?," he asked. "Well," she replied. "People held them under Jesus feet as he walked down the road." The boy was shocked. "Wouldn't you know it! The one time I miss church, Jesus shows up!"

Dear Fr. Joe,

Books such as *The Da Vinci Code* suggest the existence of writings that the church works hard to suppress. Are there other "gospels" such as the "Gnostic gospels?" What are they? Are they for real?

A fascination with these so-called gospels has been manifested in all sorts of popular culture outlets – movies, books, articles, etc. In this article, I hope to give real examples of our fascination with these writings and show a bit about where they come from.

Let's start with a popular movie, made in 1999, called *Stigmata*. I remember my students asking me to watch it and telling me how accurate it was. This thriller was about a priest who was called on by the Vatican to research a Gnostic writing, the "Gospel of Thomas." As a result of his research, he became an enemy of the church because he now knew "the truth about Jesus." He came to believe that the "Gospel of Thomas" was the authentic Gospel written by Jesus himself and that the others – Matthew, Mark, Luke and John – came afterward and were put in the Bible by the church, so the church could maintain its power.

At the end of the movie, words come up on the screen to inform the viewers that the "Gospel of Thomas" is a real document "written in Aramaic," and that "many scholars" believe it to be the real words of Jesus, written by himself.

Now, to be fair, it may be true that "many scholars" believe the "Gospel of Thomas" to be authentic, but they are certainly not biblical scholars. As a side note, the "Gospel of Thomas" wasn't written in Aramaic. It was written in Coptic, an ancient Egyptian language, which I believe used Greek symbols.

That movie promoted a lot of confusion in young people who watched it, and I believe it is along the same lines as *The Da Vinci Code* in its concepts. Both are based on the Gnostic gospels.

So what are these "gospels?"

They are the writings of a religious sect that predated Christianity by a good amount of time and is possibly rooted in Babylonian mysticism. A basic tenet of this religion is that salvation can be attained through the discovery and mastery of certain "secrets" about God, heaven, and life itself. This knowledge is not for everyone. Thus, this religion steeped itself in secrecy. Gnosticism remained "under the radar" for quite some time, and is only recently re-emerging as a factor in world religion.

So, how did this group get so involved in Christianity to the point that some of their writings were about Jesus? Well, we gotta take a history lesson here. Remember, from the beginning of the church (A.D. 33) until Christianity became legal (A.D. 314), Christianity was an illegal, underground religion. Christians had to meet after dark in secluded places and use secret signs to communicate. During this time period, different groups invaded the Christian underground and began to spread their own unique blend of their religion and Christian thought.

During this time, Christian leaders such as Origen, Clement of Alexandria and others wrote to Christians, warning them about false writings that were disguised as Christian writings. Now, I am simplifying a bit, but a key reason these leaders wrote against these Gnostic writings is because, quite literally, salvation is offered to everyone – not a select few who attain "secret knowledge."

When Christianity exploded from the underground in the early fourth century, there were innumerable Christian sects that came out of hiding and began to communicate with each other. Certain premises were universally embraced among these churches, and certain ideas were universally condemned. A council was convened at Nicea, in order to determine what was Christian and what was not. It's from this council that we get the Nicene Creed.

This council provided clarity for Christians then and today, as it informs us what the apostles passed on to their successors. Some of what is written in the Nicene Creed is a direct response to Gnosticism. As a result of this council and the success of the inclusive Christian message, Gnosticism faded away.

Let's get to the common theme in movies and books that the church has worked to suppress these gospels. At the beginning (meaning the first 300 years of Christianity), the church did work hard to fight these Gnostic writings, but lacked the political power to muscle any group out. Remember, we were the persecuted ones – not the ones doing the persecuting.

As time went on, the church didn't have to suppress the Gnostic writings. They had little to no following. Reading some of these "gospels" should easily give one the sense as to why. They are confused, convoluted and bizarre beyond reckoning. Most people who've read them have read edited versions that have removed a great deal of the "weirdness" that they contain. Stories like the one where Jesus killed children for making fun of him, and then raised them back to life at the behest of his mother, are par for the course in some of these Gnostic writings. Interspersed into these are passages that are pirated from the four Gospels that we read. Unfortunately, Hollywood handles this by dropping the bizarre in favor of the more palatable or even poetic quotes, like the one verse used over and over in *Stigmata:* "The kingdom of God is within you and all around you. It is not within buildings of wood or stone. Split a piece of wood and you will find me. Look beneath a stone and I am there." (Gospel of Thomas, v. 3)

These confused and confusing writings, coupled with their exclusive theology, doomed Gnosticism to a lifetime of obscurity. The church didn't need to work hard or send out assassins to cover these up. On my bookshelf, I have copies of all the Gnostic writings that I bought at a Catholic bookstore in 1993. Their copyright date? 1901. Why did I buy these books? I needed them for my Scripture and history classes at seminary. If the church was working hard to cover it up, they did an exceptionally lousy job.

If you want to take a look at translations of these writings, go to: *www.wesley.nnu.edu/biblical_studies/nocanon/gospils.htm.*

Warning! Bad joke ahead!

Have you heard the story about the doctor talking to a lawyer at a party? Their conversation was constantly interrupted by people asking the doctor medical questions. Finally, the doctor turned to the lawyer and asked if people were constantly peppering him with legal questions. The lawyer said "Sure, it used to be a problem, but then I started sending out bills and it quit right away." The doctor thought this was a great idea and went home from the party and wrote out a bunch of bills. When he went to put them in the mailbox the next day, he found a bill from the lawyer.

Dear Fr. Joe,

I have a Protestant friend who tells me Catholics only have nine commandments and we leave out the commandment about idols. She showed me in her Bible how we left it out. Is that true? Also, why do we have statues in churches if God says not to do it?

Nope, not true. Let's take a look at the commandment format, because the answer lies there. Turn your Bible to *Exodus 20:1-17*. You there? *Exodus*! After *Genesis* and before *Leviticus*. Got it? Good!

OK, now in the first part of the commandments, we see there are two ideas: first that we should worship God alone and second that we should not carve idols and worship them. If we then look at *verse 17*, we see again two ideas, first that we should not covet our neighbor's goods, and second that we should not covet our neighbor's wife.

So, an abbreviated version of the commandments would look like this:

1. Worship God alone; do not carve and worship idols.
2. Do not take God's name in vain.
3. Keep the Sabbath holy.
4. Honor your parents.
5. Do not kill.
6. Do not commit adultery.
7. Do not steal.
8. Do not bear false witness.
9. Do not covet your neighbor's spouse.
10. Do not covet your neighbor's goods.

That is our 10. *(cf. Deut 5:6-21)* Some translations combine the first two commandments and split the last two, others split the first two and join the last two. Some of our well-meaning Protestant brothers and sisters may have seen our list and wondered where the injunction against carving and worshiping idols is.

Now, if the commandment forbids us from carving "graven images," why do we have statues in churches? Again, let's go to the source. *Exodus 20:4-6* goes like this:

> *You shall not carve idols for yourselves in the shape of anything in the sky above or on the earth below or in the waters beneath the earth; you shall not bow down before them or worship them. For I, the Lord, your God, am a jealous God, inflicting punishment for their fathers' wickedness on the children of those who hate me, down to the third and fourth generation; but bestowing mercy down to the thousandth generation, on the children of those who love me and keep my commandments.*

So, why do we make statues? The commandment forbids the creation of images that we worship, but not the creation of holy images to help our worship. At times in the Scriptures, God commanded the creation of images and statues to help people pray. Here are a few examples:

In the ***Book of Numbers***, God has the Israelites construct a bronze serpent that they should look at when bitten by snakes so that they could be healed.

Another example comes from God giving instructions to David concerning how to build the first temple. According to the Bible, God gave David explicit instructions, which included the creation of statues of angels. (*1 Chr 28:18-19*)

In this second example, God is explaining how to decorate the tent of the Lord's presence:

> *Make two cherubim of beaten gold for the two ends of the propitiatory, fastening them so that one cherub springs direct from each end. The cherubim shall have their wings spread out above, covering the propitiatory with them; they shall be turned toward each other, but with their faces looking toward the propitiatory.* (*Ex 25:18-20*)

Now, look at ***Ezekiel 41:17-18***. Here, God is describing the construction of graven (carved) images in the future temple. God gives Ezekiel a vision and describes the walls of the temple as having carvings of angels.

On the related topic of praying to the saints, we believe that saints are people who are in heaven and standing in the sight of God. We ask them for prayers, just like we ask our friends and neighbors that we can see for prayers. We don't worship the statues. We use them to stimulate our imagination while we ask them to pray for us or when we remember their stories of faith.

I could keep going, but you get the idea. God understands that we are physical beings who need physical signs. In the same way that you and I carry around pictures of our family, we need to carry in our hearts the images of people who inspire our faith and teach us how to live.

So, go to your church, see the statues and thank God for the men and women who inspire us. For a great site on how to defend our faith, I highly recommend *www.catholic.com*. It absolutely rocks!

Dear Fr. Joe,

What do people mean when they ask if I am "born again"? I've always been Catholic – do I need to have a conversion experience and what would that look and feel like?

Everybody needs a conversion experience. Even more than that, all of us need a daily conversion experience. Well, maybe not my mother.

I think I will answer the "born again" question before breaking the previous line down, so that my answer on the conversion question will make more sense.

In your baptism, you were born again. The waters in the baptismal font are the waters of the womb of our holy mother, the church. You went in the water and emerged a new creation. At that point, your heart was directed toward God in a special way. Some other things happened, but I am focusing on your question.

So, you were born again if you were baptized. The problem is, for a great many people, there wasn't a ton of "follow through" after that. If that is the case, then you need to be "born again."

Think of it this way: Baptism gives you all the grace you need, but you have to respond to it each day in order to be fully born again. It's like someone giving me Double Stuf Oreos® – receiving them is nice, but eating them is divine.

Being born again is an expression that Jesus used to describe the process of entering into a personal relationship with him. This is when you, as an adult, make a commitment to Jesus to live the way he has called you to live.

It's called being born again because it is a rebirth – it's that moment when all our priorities change, when the way we view the world changes. We are a new creature in Christ when we are born again. We give ourselves to Jesus: heart, mind, body and soul. We give him absolute lordship in our lives. This surrender will change us radically.

When, where and how do you do it? Anywhere, anytime (though I am partial to doing this in front of the Blessed Sacrament). You get down on your knees and surrender your life to Jesus. I am not going to tell you how to pray, because you know what you need to say.

Christianity is, in my mind, first and foremost about surrender. Conversion is a huge part of this.

See, the closer we draw to Jesus, the more we realize how we have fallen short and how we continue to fall short. God understands this and meets us in our frailty, but he always, always wants us to do our best with his help.

Conversion starts when we see the gap between who we are and who we are called to be; it continues when we feel sorrow about that gap and it reaches its pinnacle when we ask God's forgiveness and help. God will fill that gap.

This process of conversion is prompted and maintained by grace, or strength from heaven, and it must be a daily event.

Dear Fr. Joe,
I've seen TV evangelists lay hands on people to "heal" them. How is this different from our sacrament of anointing the sick?

Sometimes TV evangelists make it seem as if physical healing is guaranteed if the sick person just believes – I'm not always sure if they're supposed to believe in Jesus or in the evangelist!

In any case, no person can guarantee physical healing to another person. Even the apostles experienced illness and death. What Jesus did leave us is his comfort in time of sickness and frailty – a comfort we can experience in the sacrament of anointing of the sick.

When Jesus healed the sick during his earthly ministry, he was giving us all a sign that the kingdom of God was near – that God had extended compassion to his people. That compassion is still with us today – and we are supposed to act like Jesus by comforting the sick and caring for the elderly.

Jesus used signs, like spittle and the laying on of hands, to heal those who came to him in faith. Those same signs and gestures are repeated in the anointing of the sick. The priest lays hands on the ill person, prays over them and anoints them with holy oil blessed by the bishop for this purpose. This rite comes right out of the Bible – in the early church, the apostles did the same thing. *(cf Jas 5:14-15)*

Amazing physical healings have been attributed to this sacrament, but whether or not there is a physical result, the major effect is one of spiritual healing and peace. The sacrament's particular gift is to strengthen the faith and trust of the person who's ill. It also unites the sick person to the sufferings of Jesus.

Anyone who is seriously ill, or in danger of death, or just frail from old age can receive the sacrament. And, unlike the old days when we called it extreme unction, this sacrament is not reserved for the deathbed anymore.

Anointing of the sick is not magical mumbo-jumbo, but it is an awesome gift from God.

Dear Fr. Joe,
Why is there a need for the papacy?

Let's start at the beginning. If we look at **Matthew 16:17-19**, Jesus says,

> *Blessed are you, Simon son of Jonah. For flesh and blood has not revealed this to you, but my heavenly Father. And so I say to you, you are Peter, and upon this rock I will build my church, and the gates of the netherworld shall not prevail against it. I will give you the keys to the kingdom of heaven. Whatever you bind on earth shall be bound in heaven, and whatever you loose on earth shall be loosed in heaven.*

This is the basis for having a pope. Let's take it piece by piece.

At the beginning of this passage, we see Jesus giving a specific blessing and power to Simon Peter. That blessing is rooted in the gift God gave Peter – knowledge about Jesus that the others did not have yet.

Jesus then says that Simon is now to be called Peter (the word for Peter and rock are the same in Aramaic), and that God will build his church on Peter, the rock. So, we use this passage to re-affirm our belief that God desires his people to be led by Peter and Peter's successors. This is the beginning of our teaching on the papacy.

As Catholics, this is essential to our identity: We are led by a man who is appointed by God, in love with Jesus and led by the Holy Spirit. The pope uses his authority to hold us together in unity and define Catholic theology.

Dear Fr. Joe,
What is papal infallibility and when is it invoked?

When we begin with papal authority, I find that we cannot do much better than the ***Catholic Encyclopedia***, so I am going to paraphrase it.

The ***Catholic Encyclopedia*** uses the four points of the church to justify papal authority:

- Jesus founded his church as a visible and perfect society.
- He intended everybody be a part of this church as much as possible.
- He desired that the "church be one, with a visible corporate unity of faith, government and worship."
- In order to make these things a reality, Jesus gave the Apostles and

their successors the authority to govern the people and lead them toward unity.

So, the church teaches us that Jesus intended a system of authority for his people so that we could be one, and in our unity we would show the world a positive example.

Within this concept of papal authority is a teaching that we call *ex cathedra,* a phrase we use to describe a practice. The phrase literally means "from the chair." Whenever the pope speaks *ex cathedra,* he is without error in what he says.

Now, this doesn't really have anything to do with the pope sitting in his chair and saying things; he can speak *ex cathedra* while standing, and just because he says something while he's sitting in his chair, that doesn't make it an *ex cathedra* teaching.

The pope has to declare himself to be speaking *ex cathedra,* and what he teaches has to be in union with Sacred Scripture and tradition. Examples are the doctrines regarding the Immaculate Conception and the Assumption.

As a final note, the church is clear that it is only to use its infallible teaching authority in matters of faith and morals. So, the pope cannot and will not speak infallibly about matters that are not issues of faith and morals.

Warning! Bad joke ahead!

A bishop called in one of his priests and said, "While celebrating Mass the other day, I noticed that you changed the words of the eucharistic prayer. Instead of saying, "We pray for our bishop," you say, "We pray for our bishop, God's unworthy servant." The priest was shocked, saying "Well, Excellency, that is what you say when you get to that part. It sounded so humble and beautiful, I thought I should say it, too. Why is it OK for you to refer to yourself as an unworthy servant, but wrong for me to refer to you that way?"

The bishop paused and said, "Well, because when you say it, you mean it ... "

How does the church choose bishops?

This was a great question for me! I stared at it for a long time and realized I really had no idea how it is done. I researched and found some great stuff, but none was more helpful than: *http://frpat.com/bishopchoice.htm*. It is a fantastic resource, and most of my information for this will come from that site.

The first point Father Pat makes is that the Holy Spirit makes the choice. I like that. It would be too easy to simply delve into the process while forgetting the most important part. We believe the Holy Spirit guides the church in a holy and special way. We can trust that Jesus does not leave his flock abandoned, thank God!

Finding the right priest begins with the bishop of a region submitting names of priests with the right gifts to the local metropolitan bishop. The next step is when the bishops of an area meet with their metropolitan and make a list to give to the papal nuncio. The papal nuncio is someone the pope appoints to do two things:

- Serve as the ambassador to a country, and
- Represent the pope for all the Catholics in that country.

The papal nuncio for the U.S. is an Italian archbishop who checks out the priests on the list – he prays and discerns to identify their strengths and weaknesses. The priests' friends and family receive a confidential form to fill out to assist in Archbishop Sambi's investigation. The result of this process is that the nuncio has a solid understanding of the various priests whom the bishops consider good prospects for the episcopacy. This way, when a diocese opens up, the nuncio can send the Congregation for Bishops in Rome a shorter list of priests whose particular gifts and talents will fit that diocese best.

When the Congregation of Bishops receives the list, they pray about it and discuss it together. The end result is that they send the pope an even shorter list. The pope sits down with the congregation and the nuncio to pray and discuss who the Holy Spirit is calling them to appoint.

Now, as I understand it, neither the papal nuncio nor the pope are slaves to this list: They can choose whomever they feel the Spirit is calling them to appoint.

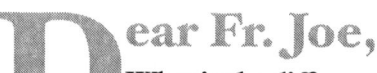

Dear Fr. Joe,
What is the difference between Catholic Communion and Protestant Communion? May I receive Communion in a Protestant church?

We have to start off with a really basic idea – there are literally tens of thousands of Protestant denominations and there are about that many different ideas among them about what Communion is. For example, many

Episcopalians believe in the real presence of Jesus in the Eucharist, but some don't. Missouri Synod Lutherans believe in the real presence, but in a different way than we do. I could go on, but I think you get the idea.

It's easier to say what we believe. We believe the Eucharist is primarily two things: reality and a sign.

- Reality: we believe the Eucharist is the very flesh and blood of Jesus Christ, the Son of God. We believe that the bread still looks and tastes like bread. In philosophy, that appearance is called the accident. However, we believe that the essence of the bread is replaced by Jesus. Philosophically, we call this the substance. In the end, the bread is permanently transformed into Jesus. This process is called transubstantiation. What a word!

- Sign: The Eucharist is a sign of our unity with the church. It's also the source of that unity, but that is another article. When we receive the Eucharist, we are saying that we are in communion with the church. We are indicating that we have surrendered our will (not intellect) to the wisdom of the church, as passed on to us through the successors of the apostles, our bishops. I guess an easy way to say it is this — when we are in communion with the church and struggle with a teaching of the church, we assume we need to change.

When we go with our Protestant brothers and sisters to church, we should refrain from receiving Communion precisely because we are not yet in full communion with them. Tragically, the prayer of Jesus in ***John 15*** that we "be one," as Jesus is one with the Father and the Holy Spirit, isn't here yet. We are divided, and a sad consequence of that division is that we can't receive a sign of unity.

Let's continue to pray that we who profess to believe in Christ will grow in unity and "be one."

Warning! Bad joke ahead!

A friend of mine recently pointed out to me the dramatic proof that there were cars in Biblical times. It's true! Enjoy these examples:

In Genesis, we learn that God drove Adam and Eve out of the Garden in a Fury. In Kings and Chronicles, we find that David's Triumph was heard throughout the land. Even the New Testament offers us some proofs — look at the book of Acts; it tells us that the apostles were all in one Accord. Finally, 2 Corinthians, verse 48 describes traveling in a Volkswagen Beetle – "We are pressed in every way, but not cramped beyond movement."

I think you all burned off minutes in purgatory just by reading that ...

Dear Fr. Joe,
How do people who are allergic to wheat receive Communion?

Some people are allergic to wheat and some have Celiac disease, which means they are gluten-intolerant. When it's time to receive Communion, our brothers and sisters with these conditions can have trouble receiving the host because the only two ingredients allowed in making the bread are wheat and water – that is it. They may find themselves unable to receive the sacred body of Christ. They are, however, generally able to receive the precious blood. The church defines this using the principle of the hypostatic union. That term basically means that, even as Jesus' full humanity and divinity were present in him, both the sacred body and the precious blood contain the fullness of the Eucharistic experience. Those who receive only the blood are not getting "less than" those who are able to receive both species. Your pastor can explain this in more detail if you'd like.

For example, in our diocese, there are several options open to those who suffer from gluten intolerance, or Celiac disease. The church understands that Celiac sufferers can be seriously harmed by ingesting even a small amount of gluten, and has taken steps to accommodate their needs:

- A low-gluten host, made by the Benedictine Sisters in Missouri, should be available in all parishes. Its gluten content is 0.01 percent. Check with your physician first, and then inform the pastor prior to Mass that you will need the low-gluten host. The pastor should be familiar with safe handling of these hosts: consecrating them in a separate pyx, refraining from handling them after he's touched other bread and ensuring they do not come in contact with wheat-containing products.

- If you cannot have any gluten at all, you may receive the precious blood from the cup. In order to avoid wheat contamination, you can bring a sterilized chalice from home. The chalice should be stored in a zip-top plastic bag until it is filled with wine. After filling, the priest will ensure that no bread is placed into it during the fraction rite. Make arrangements with your pastor ahead of time.

Chapter Two: Questions about the church

Dear Fr. Joe,
If I don't like my priest, can I switch parishes?

First of all, I think it's important to keep in mind that you are not enslaved to any location for attending Mass. Although parishes are defined geographically, you may participate in another parish's worship and activities. In some dioceses, you may register in a parish of your choosing; in others, your registration is restricted to the parish where you are technically a member – which is the parish in which you reside. Under canon law, whether you register or not, you are a member of that parish. I know my family drove 45 minutes to go to a church because the priest there was an incredibly holy, rare man and we didn't want to miss out on that gift. That helped my spirituality immensely.

I do think it's important to go to the Catholic parish that feeds your soul best. A buddy of mine commuted a significant distance to his church and had a bumper sticker that said, "A church alive is worth the drive!" That sums it up well.

I believe that our reasons for switching parishes or not switching are important. If we are switching because Mass is shorter somewhere else, I think that is a bad idea. God deserves our time, talents and energy – basing our worship on how quickly we can get out sends our souls a bad message.

Switching parishes is a big deal and shouldn't be taken lightly. Make sure that you pray and talk this through with friends before making your choice. Trust that the Holy Spirit will guide your open heart.

Dear Fr. Joe,
My friend's mom can speak in tongues and sometimes demonstrates this for us. It seems pretty weird and I'm not sure I believe it's anything other than gibberish. What's the deal with that?

OK, let's look at what the gift of tongues is. In **Romans 8, verse 26**, Paul says:

In the same way, the Spirit too comes to the aid of our weakness; for we do not know how to pray as we ought, but the Spirit itself intercedes with inexpressible groanings.

The beginning of *1 Corinthians 14* is almost entirely dedicated to the issue of tongues as well and is worth reading.

What is the idea, then? That sometimes, in prayer, our souls hunger for God and proximity to God is so intense that it begins to speak through us. When someone is speaking in tongues, the Spirit is speaking through them to others. It ends up sounding like "gibberish" to those nearby, but it is anything but.

Not everyone is called to speak in tongues and you honestly don't need to be totally comfortable with it, but you should accept that it is a real gift that some have.

In terms of someone demonstrating it for you, I'm not sure how I feel about that. *I Corinthians 14:2* states:

For one who speaks in a tongue does not speak to human beings but to God, for no one listens; he utters mysteries in spirit.

Paul goes on to say that not only is the person speaking only to God, but that they are not to do it to "build themselves up." Finally in *verse 9* of the same chapter, Paul asks,

Similarly, if you, because of speaking in tongues, do not utter intelligible speech, how will anyone know what is being said? For you will be talking to the air.

Now, lest we get "down on" tongues, in *verse 18*, Paul thanks God that he speaks in tongues "more than anybody."

So, in the end, when it comes to tongues, Paul wants us all to be balanced. We need to recognize that the gift of tongues is a movement of the Spirit and thus is sacred. We should treat it as such and honor those who have the gift and those who have it need to treat it with respect.

Dear Fr. Joe,

What is a "charismatic" Catholic?

Well, you are reading the words of one right now, so I think I can help on this one!

The simplest explanation is this: A charismatic is a Catholic who is open to receiving and acting on the gifts of the Spirit in an overt way.

OK, first of all, we need to clarify something. As I described what a charismatic Catholic is, some of you might have thought, "Well, all of us should be that," and you are right. To some extent, it's inaccurate for us to speak as if some Catholics are called to be open to the Spirit and others aren't.

Look at this great passage from the book of ***Romans (12:3–8)***:

For by the grace given to me I tell everyone among you not to think of himself more highly than one ought to think, but to think soberly, each according to the measure of faith that God has apportioned. For as in one body we have many parts, and all the parts do not have the same function, so we, though many, are one body in Christ and individually parts of one another. Since we have gifts that differ according to the grace given to us, let us exercise them: if prophecy, in proportion to the faith; if ministry, in ministering; if one is a teacher, in teaching; if one exhorts, in exhortation; if one contributes, in generosity; if one is over others, with diligence; if one does acts of mercy, with cheerfulness.

Here Paul is pointing out that God has blessed the body of Christ (the church) with many diverse and wonderful gifts that can strengthen us and unite us to work together for the spread of the Gospel.

A charismatic focuses part of his or her prayer on receiving the gifts of the Spirit he or she needs in order to carry out God's mission on earth. The Spirit can prompt us to be where we need to be and strengthen us to do what we need to do. If you've ever read the New Testament and wondered why we weren't doing those same things, it's because we've forgotten to be empowered by the Holy Spirit.

The simple prayer, "Come Holy Spirit," can be the beginning. Ask around your parish for someone who can guide you into activating the gift of the Spirit you received in your baptism and confirmation.

Dear Fr. Joe,

Is there such a thing as an "orthodox" Catholic (as opposed to Greek Orthodox)? I gather it's a term that implies people are "conservative" Catholics. I heard someone use this expression, but I didn't know there were different degrees or versions of Catholicism.

Great question…it's funny how often we are not careful with our terminology or fail to explain it and, as a result, confusion and chaos ensue.

The ***Catholic Encyclopedia*** gives us a great explanation:

[Orthodox is] the technical name for the body of Christians who use the Byzantine Rite in various languages and are in union with the Patriarch of Constantinople but

in schism with the Pope of Rome. The epithet Orthodox (orthodoxos), meaning "right believer," is, naturally, claimed by people of every religion. It is almost exactly a Greek form of the official title of the chief enemies of the Greeks, i.e., the Muslims (mu'min, fidelis). The Monophysite Armenians called themselves ughapar, meaning exactly the same thing.

We'll take this one step at a time.

Let's start with councils. When we say the church had a council, we are referring to a large gathering of bishops that get together to resolve big issues of the day or big questions confronting Christianity. Vatican II, for example, is one of our councils. Now, when we talk about our Orthodox brothers and sisters, we are talking about a group that accepts the earliest councils in Christianity, but who separated from the Church of Rome before later councils. I think it fair to say that, in most cases, our Orthodox brothers and sisters are with us on everything except where Jesus intended our authority to lie. For us Roman Catholics, it lies with the Pope of Rome. For the Orthodox, authority lies with the patriarch of a different place. We are, literally, out of communion with our Orthodox brothers and sisters in this case.

Why we broke apart has to do with cultural clashes as well as some religious disputes. Most would agree that the key and most tragic moment in all of this came with the sacking of Constantinople by Roman Catholics in 204. The division intensified that day and some feel the wounds will never be healed.

This, in a nutshell, is a description of Orthodox as a religious group.

On top of this, within Catholicism, you do find people who refer to themselves as either "orthodox" or striving to be so. I'm one of 'em! What does this mean?

Well, again, if you look at the definition from the **Catholic Encyclopedia**, you see that orthodox literally means "right believer" or "pure worship." In the Catholic world, this is a word some people use to describe how they follow the teachings of Christ.

As a general rule, those who are of a more traditional bent tend to use it to designate the degree with which they are in union with the Church of Rome. In this case, the simple and short explanation is that a person using the word in this context is referring to their concern that they be obedient to what the church says in a literal sense.

Also, as a general rule, those of a more progressive bent tend to use it to designate the degree with which they are in union with what they perceive as the ideals behind the teachings from Rome. Again, the simple and short explanation is that a person who uses the term orthodox in this case is referring to his or her obedience to "the spirit of the words."

In case you were wondering, we need both. I remember in seminary one of the bishops put it this way: "We've got people in left field and people in right field. I'm just happy they're playin' ball."

I like that. We all should strive to follow Christ as best we can and ditch any prejudice against people who are striving as hard as we are but in a different way. I don't mean that we passively sit back and allow people to make what we believe to be grievous errors, not at all. I mean that if we feel called to challenge a fellow believer in Christ about his or her theology, we do it in a spirit of love and humility.

Jesus gave us one commandment above all: Love one another.

Dear Fr. Joe,
Did the priest scandals prove that a celibate priesthood is unrealistic?

I say this with all the sincerity I have: The time of the priest scandal was, and I think will always be, among the worst times of most priests' lives. Its effects continue today as we struggle with helping those who were wounded heal; the re-establishment of our moral authority; our trust in the bishops; and rebuilding the image of priests.

What did it teach us? So much, and yet we have so much more to learn. I believe it taught us to, in the words of one of my heroes, "Listen to the voice of the Shepherd before we listen to any other voice." It taught us that we must always be open with our failings and faults. It taught us that despite its incessant mocking or attacking of Christianity, society does hold us to a higher standard.

The scandal also taught us that people will stoop quite low in their efforts to change the church into their image and likeness. Some people, while bemoaning the fate of those injured by sexual abuse, proceeded to use these victims again – this time, to promote their own cause.

In the end, one of the other results of this crisis is the fact that we are asking good questions such as yours: Does the scandal teach us that celibate priesthood doesn't work or is unrealistic?

Mental health professionals say "no." In fact, if you look at some statistics, you will see that Catholic priests are less likely as a group to engage in sexual abuse of minors than a great deal of other professions.

The issue for most isn't just that minors were abused, but that the church authorities didn't deal with it properly and in a spirit of openness.

Be this as it may, priestly celibacy is definitely being questioned and even attacked. I think this is a good time to explain some of the reasons why we priests are celibate.

Father Cantalemessa was Pope John Paul II's private preacher, and he gave a retreat a few years ago for the priests of our diocese. In that retreat, he offered us some beautiful reflections on priestly celibacy and I'll try to represent them well here.

First of all, priestly celibacy is to be seen as a prophesy. In **Matthew 19, verses 10–13**, Jesus has just answered a question about divorce:

> [His] disciples said to him, "If that is the case of a man with his wife, it is better not to marry." He answered, "Not all can accept [this] word, but only those to whom that is granted. Some are incapable of marriage because they were born so; some, because they were made so by others; some, because they have renounced marriage for the sake of the kingdom of heaven. Whoever can accept this ought to accept it."

Here, Jesus is reminding us that some people can and should renounce marriage for the sake of heaven.

Priestly celibacy can be a prophesy to the world; we priests are called with our celibacy to literally use our hearts and even our sexuality to proclaim to the world that all this is temporary, that the kingdom of heaven is, in fact, at hand. We tie ourselves to nothing on earth, that we can assist other people and ourselves in focusing on heaven.

Another reason we priests embrace celibacy is that in it, we imitate Christ who did not marry. I know there is a lot of popular myth that attempts to convince us otherwise, but if you take a look at the Gospels and the letters of the apostles, you see an accurate source of information that isn't writing and speculating through culturally biased eyes, but was written by people who were actually there. John reminds us in **1 John, chapter 1** that he was there and is telling us the truth. In this case, we know Jesus wasn't married and thus was celibate. With our priesthood, we priests are connecting ourselves with Jesus in a special way.

There's a lot more, but I'm running out of space. Let me just say that I thank God for the gift of priestly celibacy. I feel so honored in my heart to be a priest. I know that people are struggling with trusting the priesthood right now and I encourage you to see us as you see yourselves – faulty men who are doing their best to love and serve God and God's people.

I thank Jesus with all my heart for letting me be a priest.

Chapter Two: Questions about the church

Dear Fr. Joe,
Is yoga a religion? Can you do yoga and be Catholic?

You know, the funny thing is, you are basically asking for the "Catholic position on yoga." Ouch; that one was bad.

Anyway, your question has some curious timing for me. I've been struggling for a bit with my health – fatigue and muscle soreness from football injuries. The long and short of it is, not too long ago I went to my doctor and was given some stretches. I had been doing them for over a month and was amazed at how these stretches helped. One of my buddies came to visit who had been struggling with the same kinds of issues that I was. When I showed him the stretches, he told me they were "yoga stretches." I checked it out, and sure enough, five of the eight stretches I was doing were yoga.

At the same time, I have received more than a few questions like this and I've spent some time hunting this down and hope that my answer is helpful.

When I looked, I found a flat out dogfight on the Internet about all this and, as near as I can figure, the idea is this: Yogic stretches are okay, but yoga philosophy is a problem.

This Rock, a solid Catholic apologetics site *(http://www.catholic.com/thisrock/2001/0107qq.asp)*, put it best:

"Two factors are relevant here: First, it depends on whether the yoga is being presented in a manner that is free of religious elements – i.e., purely as a system of physical exercise. If it is coupled with elements of Hindu spirituality (e.g., talk about moving kundalini, or energy, around your body), it is not appropriate for Catholics to use it as part of their exercise routine."

In summary, if you are doing stretches to help your body, then that is good, as your body is sacred and unique in creation, but with these stretches, a philosophy is often offered that is not good. Yoga stretches? Good. Yoga philosophy/religion? Not so good.

So, you may ask, "What is the problem with Hinduism?" Well, there are more than a few, but we will cover some of the bigger ones.

At this point, you gotta remember, the Catholic Church is a big believer in something we call "absolute truth." I got this definition of absolute truth from, of all places, a Web site called *"absolutetruth.net"*:

"[Absolute Truth is the belief that] there are absolute realities, or standards, that define what is real and what is not. Thus, actions can be deemed right or wrong based upon how they measure up against absolute standards."

As Catholics, we are big on this. The key idea is that in every thought and action there is right and wrong. When we talk about God and how we relate to him, there are ideas that work and are right, and there are ideas that don't work and are wrong. There are some practices that are "more right" than others and some that are "more wrong" than others. This is essential to the Catholic belief and worldview and Hinduism teaches this is incorrect. In Hinduism, there are many paths to God; in Christianity, Jesus is "The way, the truth and the life." *(Jn 14:6)*

Another problem with Hinduism is the belief in reincarnation: the belief that there is a pool of souls, and that we are reborn again and again in different forms and persons until we get it right. This idea is completely incompatible with Christianity. The **Book of Hebrews** tells us that we "die once" and then the judgment follows. *(Heb 9:27)* Also, there is a problem here with focusing on the human ability to "get it right" without divine help. We need Jesus and the power of the Holy Spirit, not numerous chances to get to heaven.

I think it best to close this section with a quote from Pope John Paul II from his document **Tertio Millennio Adveniente**:

> *How are we to imagine a life beyond death? Some have considered various forms of reincarnation: depending on one's previous life, one would receive a new life in either a higher or lower form, until full purification is attained. This belief, deeply rooted in some Eastern religions, itself indicates that man rebels against the finality of death. He is convinced that his nature is essentially spiritual and immortal.*

This is just a glimpse of some of the problems with Hinduism, but I feel compelled to remind that simply because we disagree with someone, we should never disrespect or mock them. If God calls us to speak the truth in love, then we do so, without condemnation or self-righteousness. We can disagree with someone and love him or her, as Jesus did.

In fact, that is precisely what we are supposed to do.

Dear Fr. Joe,

Do people go right to heaven or wait until the end of time?

Well, assuming they "make the cut"...

In a nutshell, we believe that immediately upon death, a person stands before God in what we call "particular judgment." At that point, his or her soul will go to purgatory, heaven, or hell, while the natural processes begin to occur in the body. Then, when Jesus returns, there will be another judgment and, wherever we are, our bodies will join our souls there, though in a different form than they are now.

Where do we get all this? From our two best sources: Sacred Scripture and sacred tradition.

In **Hebrews 9:27**, it says, "And it is appointed that each man die once, but after this comes the judgment." At the moment of death, each of us will look at God face to face and we will be judged. I think it's easiest to think of it this way: our whole lives are a process of coming to know Jesus better or not and when we see Jesus, if we have a relationship with him, we will, to paraphrase the words of Jesus, "know each other."

This is a key idea. I think, too often, we pretend that if we are "good" or "nice" then we will be instantly "saved." That's not at all how Jesus presents it. I think it was Father Rohr who pointed out that Jesus never once used the word "nice." Instead, each of us needs to commit to following Jesus daily and allowing him to guide us. We need to spend time with Jesus in prayer every day and grow in our knowledge of who Jesus is and what that means. If our ideas of love and wisdom aren't growing and changing daily, we can take that as a sign that we are not growing in our relationship with Jesus. All along the way, the sacraments are there to help, guide, and strengthen us in this relationship so that we can be who we are called to be.

If we've nourished this relationship with Jesus, then when we see him, we will know him, and at that point, enter into what we call "purgatory."

I know there are a lot of bad ideas out there about purgatory, but I have a way to explain it that might help. Don't think of purgatory as a separate place from heaven, but as a part of heaven. (People who go to purgatory are definitely going to heaven.) Think of it like this: If you come into a crowded room and I'm on the other side, then it will take you a bit to get to me. That process of you drawing closer to me is like the experience of purgatory. (Notice in this model I'm God? That may very well be why I like this model so much.) Either way, as we draw close to God, all the ways that we've damaged our souls are slowly healed by the fire of God's presence. All that is impure in us and distorted is burned away by the fire of God's love. It hurts, but it's a good hurt, a weight room burn, as it were.

I digress.

When Jesus returns, we "wrap up" the whole thing. Those who are in heaven or hell stay there at the second coming of Christ. Those in purgatory enter heaven. At this point, all those who are alive during this time experience their particular judgment as well as general or "final judgment." This is when we will see our lives and the lives of every person in the light of God's mercy, love, and justice; in other words, it will all make sense at this moment.

All will then experience the reuniting of the body and soul in whatever place they reside at this point. Those who were judged in the final judgment will go to heaven, hell, or purgatory and we will be complete – body and soul with or away from God.

Our bodies will be, in the words of Scripture, "glorified," so they'll probably look nothing like mine at this point in my life. What does that mean? We're not exactly sure, although when Jesus was in his glorified body, people didn't recognize him without help.

This is why we have so many rules about our bodies, by the way. They are not just shells or useless containers; they are sacred and holy and destined for eternity.

In the words of Paul, let's "glorify God in our bodies" and let the Holy Spirit guide us into a deeper relationship with him in this life, so that we can be with him forever in the next.

Dear Fr. Joe,
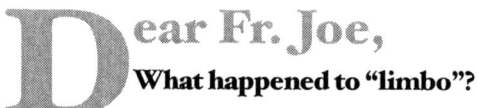
What happened to "limbo"?

I think it's near Poughkeepsie, N.Y., now ... next to the Ramada. OK, that was just wrong. I know.

So, what happened to limbo? I found a great article on this by Gerald Faggin in *America* magazine. He really breaks it down well. I am going to use his article as a guide.

The key issue is this: as our early Christian brothers and sisters worked through their understanding of God – his love and grace – they formed theories and ideas about, for lack of a better phrase, "How it all works."

When discussing baptism, our early Christian leaders recognized how important it is; Jesus made baptism a part of every commission in each Gospel. In **Matthew 28:19**, for example, Jesus puts it this way:

Go, therefore, and make disciples of all nations, baptizing them in the name of the Father, and of the Son and of the Holy Spirit.

Taking their cues from Jesus' words and the inspiration of the Holy Spirit, our earliest teachers who wrote the Bible emphasized how essential baptism was for salvation. There are many examples of this *(1 Pt 3:21; cf. Acts 2:38, 22:16, Rom 6:3-4, Col 2:11-12)*, but I think the clearest is this:

> *How can we who died to sin yet live in it? Or are you unaware that we who were baptized into Christ Jesus were baptized into his death? We were indeed buried with him through baptism into death, so that, just as Christ was raised from the dead by the glory of the Father, we too might live in newness of life.* **(Rom 6:2-4)**

As they wrestled with the necessity of baptism for salvation, they also bumped into an issue of key importance: free will. In this case, free will is our ability to say "yes" or "no" to Jesus and is essential to any question of salvation.

The next concept in all of this was heaven: people who never had an opportunity to say "no" to Jesus obviously never had a chance to say "yes" either. Although Jesus won't condemn anyone who never had a chance to know him, the early Christians believed that if we can't say "yes" to Jesus, then we cannot enter heaven.

This led, then, to the question of babies who died before baptism: since they couldn't exercise their free will and refuse or embrace baptism, what happened to them?

Our earliest answers were frankly not our best, but eventually, the idea of free choice and the importance of baptism merged in this concept that was called "limbo." The revered **Baltimore Catechism** put it this way:

> *Persons, such as infants, who have not committed actual sin and who, through no fault of theirs, die without baptism, cannot enter heaven; but it is the common belief they will go to some place similar to limbo, where they will be free from suffering, though deprived of the happiness of heaven.* **(Q.632)**

The odd thing is, you really can't find anything in church documents about this, and even our **Baltimore Catechism** specifies it as "the common belief." This is one of those situations where the church didn't give us specific direction, so we began teaching our speculation as fact.

Today, it's hard to pin down where the church is on this whole thing, as the **Catechism of the Catholic Church** doesn't even mention it. There are those who, like Faggin, believe this is because the church no longer finds the idea of limbo acceptable. I know in all my time at seminary, we weren't taught anything about limbo being part of Catholic theology now. The church can't retract any statement about limbo, because it never made one.

This doesn't mean God "changed"; God doesn't change, but what we can handle does. In the same way that kids learn more and more about their folks over time, we learn more and more about God as time goes on. God's tender love and compassion stretch beyond our imagination and we can and must always take comfort in that.

Warning! Bad joke ahead!

I heard a great story about a fourth-grade teacher telling her class that the story of Jonah is impossible. The teacher said that there is no fish with a big enough throat to swallow a person. One of the students in class argued with the teacher saying that the story of Jonah is true. So, the teacher said "Well, you are going to have to prove it." The student said that she would ask Jonah when she got to heaven. The teacher smiled and said "Well, what if Jonah isn't in heaven?" The student thought for a minute and said, "Then you can ask him."

Dear Fr. Joe,
Can I use Ouija boards, crystals and enneagrams?

OK, these are three totally different things, so first, let's define each one and then look at what they purport to do from a Catholic perspective.

First, let's look at Ouija boards. According to Princeton's Wordnet, they are boards with the alphabet on it; used with a planchette to spell out supernatural messages.

Apparently, the name comes from combining the French word for "Yes" (Oui) and the German word for "Yes" (Ja).

In terms of crystals, I assume you are asking about the way some people claim to use crystals for spiritual protection or channeling, or in any religious way.

The enneagram is a nine-sided shape that is used as a model for different things; the most common being its use as a personality assessment tool. This assessment tool focuses on the imbalance present in each person – their "hidden self." Integration is essential in this model, and each personality type is shown the way to integration through the use of arrows.

OK, we've got them now; let's take it one at a time.

The Ouija board was introduced as a board game, and was intended to be used as a way to contact the spirits of angels, demons, or the dead. This is a dangerous practice. People have approached me about this and expressed their concern over my "hard-line stance on a board game," but that is precisely one of the big problems here: disguising a fundamentally evil spiritual practice into a game for kids is, in my mind, the definition of evil.

Take a look at this passage:

> *Let there not be found among you anyone who immolates his son or daughter in the fire, nor a fortune-teller, soothsayer, charmer, diviner, or caster of spells, nor one who consults ghosts and spirits or seeks oracles from the dead. Anyone who does such things is an abomination to the Lord.* (Dt 18:10–12a)

The Scripture is clear, and many exorcists in the Catholic Church speak very strongly against the Ouija board. Whether we intend it for "fun" or not is irrelevant; it's a loaded spiritual gun and we should destroy any of these things that are in our home.

Crystals are a little harder to nail down, as they are used in so many ways. However, the simple answer is this: I can't find any circumstance under which a person can or should "use crystals" for a spiritual purpose. Again, its purpose seems quite clearly against the Scripture passage that I cited above.

The easiest way to look at these things is to remember the story of Babel and the story of Adam and Eve. In both cases, what the people wanted was right, but they wanted to do it in their own way and not in the way God calls us to. The desire to have contact with the divine is holy and good, but we must do it in the way God invites us to. The problem is when we act as if our actions can somehow "force God's hand" or as if the Scriptures and the guidance of the church aren't sufficient.

There are tons of fights on the Internet about enneagrams. Some people see them as helpful tools, others see them as an evil New Age practice. It appears that in this case, it's best to avoid working with this model. Why?

First, because of its roots. The roots of this practice appear to come from the Sufis, who seem to combine Islam and paganism in their worship.

Second, this model is a problem because of its focus on self-improvement through purely human means. In the mind of the church, it is essential that we base all of our efforts for "self improvement" on the person of Jesus Christ and the power of the Holy Spirit. One source I read indicated that Jesus calls us to "die to self," while this model calls us to an almost obsessive focus on the self.

Remember, brothers and sisters, Jesus has given us all we need to come to him. As he said in ***John 14:6,***

> *I am the way, the truth and the life. No one comes to the Father except through me.*

Dear Fr. Joe,

Can I believe in Wicca and still be Catholic? I think I can since Wicca honors nature. What do you think?

What do I think? What I think isn't really worth much. I mean, whenever someone asks me what I think about something, this is what comes to mind: If I give you my opinion based on my own experiences, you have gained little, if anything at all. Why am I saying all this? Because this attitude goes right to the heart of the answer to your question. Here is what I mean.

The Catholic Church is a 2,000-year-old institution that is blessed by God in a special way to lead people to and in Christ. In those 2,000 years, we have engaged every culture that has existed during this time. We have done beautiful things, made terrible mistakes and we have learned much. Because of this, I submit myself to the wisdom of the Catholic Church. I understand that I am not in charge. I understand that in order to be Christ-like, I need to humble myself and not seek my own power.

Why am I saying this if the question is about witchcraft? Because the issue of humility and submission are two of the places where witchcraft is an offense against God. Let's take it apart.

First of all, let's define witchcraft. When I say witchcraft, I am talking about the practice of Wiccans and other things like using Ouija boards, consulting horoscopes, going to fortune tellers, etc., OK? The church, without exception, condemns all of these practices. Look at your *catechism, sections 2115-2117*.

See, the problem is, in these practices, we take God's job away from him. We try to claim God's power over the future. For example, in trying to predict our future or have someone predict it for us, we are trying to take control over something that is not ours to control! You are God's own precious possession and all you and I need to know about the future is that God is there. The future is not ours to know or control. It is God's.

In casting spells, we run into the problem of trying to manipulate the spirit world. You cast spells and do different things to get what you want. This is not how we deal with God. God is in charge. He is not manipulated and we can't "force his hand." As Christians, we should not seek to be in charge, we should try to humble ourselves and be under God's authority.

Now, let's talk turkey. Witchcraft exposes us to a dangerous element of the spirit world. For some reason, all kinds of TV shows and movies have popped up which try to make witchcraft look fun, acceptable, harmless or even good. This is not the case.

Witchcraft is a practice that is dangerous and alienates us from God. We have to understand something very important and basic to our faith: as Catholics, heck, even as Christians, we believe that there are two beings out there that want us with them. One of them is God who loves us and desires great things for us. *(Jn 10:10)* The other is the devil and he wants us dead. *(I Pt 5:8)*

Whether we believe it or not, witchcraft brings contact with evil spirits. They may appear to be good, or even do nice things, but the problem is they only want our deaths. That is why I am being more serious in this article than usual. I don't want anyone reading this to get mixed up in it.

Please understand witchcraft is not "contacting God in a different way." God has strictly forbidden the practice. Witchcraft is not harmless or good, it is using evil spirits who appear to be good to get what we want, and that is not holy. If you are engaging in practices of witchcraft, I urge you to step away from them and pray for help. See your priest and ask him for guidance.

God loves us. We can trust him to give us what we need and help us discover what we want. God is in charge of the future and, by humbly placing ourselves in his hands, we don't need special powers from Wiccan practices and we don't need to know the future.

Warning! Bad joke ahead!

A boy was overheard talking to himself as he strode through his back yard, baseball cap in place and toting ball and bat. "I'm the greatest baseball player in the world," he said proudly. Then he tossed the ball in the air, swung and missed. Undaunted, he picked up the ball, threw it into the air and said to himself, "I'm the greatest baseball player ever!" He swung at the ball again, and again he missed. He paused a moment to examine the bat and ball carefully. Then once again he threw the ball into the air and said, "I'm the greatest baseball player who ever lived." He swung the bat hard and again missed the ball. "Wow!" he exclaimed. "What a pitcher!"

Smart answers & bad jokes

Chapter 3
Questions about relationships, emotions and values

A man was driving down a muddy country road and got stuck. He paid a passing farmer $50 to pull his car out with a tractor. After the car was back on dry ground, the motorist said to the farmer, "At those prices, I should think you would be pulling people out of the mud night and day."

"Can't," replied the farmer. "At night, I haul in water for the hole."

Dear Fr. Joe,

There's a couple at church who live together but are not married. Is it my responsibility to tell them they cannot receive Communion? Should I alert the pastor to this situation?

This is one of those good, practical questions that is a result of living in community – so, let's get right to it.

Let's be clear: By living together, this couple may be committing a mortal sin, which places their souls in danger. What you want to figure out is how to handle this in a way that will ultimately help them the most. Christians often tend to mess this up; we forget that it's about presenting the truth and beauty of the Gospel in such a way that it helps the person. I've had complete strangers approach me as a priest and tell me of my sins, and I confess I didn't sense they were correcting me out of love. This may or may not have been the case, but because we had no relationship, they had little credibility. I didn't know how to read them, so their words were not helpful.

So, the first thing to consider is your relationship with the person. In the end, the question about what to do becomes more about how well you know them. If you don't know them well, then this is one of those situations where your job is to pray and leave the rest to God, unless these folks specifically ask you for your opinion (but we just decided you don't know them that well, so I'm thinking they won't do this!).

However, if you know this couple well, you have a perfect opportunity to share with them, in love, your concerns. Start by asking questions; you and I are assuming that there is sexual activity in their relationship. There is a possibility (though I confess it is slim) that they are living as brother and sister after having discussed it with their spiritual leaders. If that is not the case, you can gently let them know how you feel they are damaging their souls. If it is a money issue, perhaps you can offer to help. Share your experience of marriage and commitment and how living together can undermine that.

In terms of the pastor, he really can't do much about the couple living together. Canon law is pretty strict concerning a person's right to a good reputation, and if someone is denied Communion, a lot of folks will ask why. The guideline we were given at seminary was that the sin must be public, persistent and grave in order for us to deny Communion. It is also extremely prudent for the priest to check with his bishop before doing such a thing.

It is always going to be a balancing act for us Christians – keeping an eye on our own sinfulness is a substantial enough job; adding the weight of other people's sins can be too much. We do run the risk of coming across as self-righteous, and in fact, we run the risk of actually becoming self-righteous. It is important that we pray for God to guide us, and that we balance confrontation, encouragement and self-knowledge.

Warning! Bad joke ahead!

Four high-school boys afflicted with spring fever skipped morning classes. After lunch, they reported to the teacher that they had a flat tire. Much to their relief, she smiled and said: "Well, you missed a test today so take seats apart from one another and take out a piece of paper."

Still smiling, she waited for them to sit down. Then she said, "Question No. 1: Which tire was flat?"

Chapter Three: Questions about relationships, emotions and values

Dear Fr. Joe,

I am really confused about forgiveness. I know we are supposed to forgive everyone, but does that mean I have to stay in the relationship? My marriage counselor is telling me something different. Please help.

Wow, great question and tough issue. The amazing thing is, I just had this discussion with some of my students and he was so relieved by what I am about to tell you. I hope and pray this helps. I am going to take you through three steps in this answer, and they look something like this:

1. We are to forgive always and everywhere.

2. While we are always called to forgive, we may not be called to reconcile.

3. Forgiveness is a process, not a moment.

OK, we must always forgive. Jesus, by his word and example, demands this of us; he doesn't suggest it. The *catechism* gives us some great words on this subject in *sections 2840 and 2845*. In it, the church reminds us that if we don't forgive others, we harden our hearts to the ability to receive forgiveness. Interestingly enough, we also learn in this section that something that can help us be more forgiving is to receive forgiveness in the sacrament of reconciliation ourselves, but we'll get into that later.

Section 2845 reminds us that God's power to forgive is without limit, which should give us hope. When we have trouble forgiving, we can call upon the strength from heaven that is being offered to us each moment by God.

Now, while we are called to forgive, we may not always be called to reconcile. To forgive someone means, in one sense, to let go of her power to control us. Reconciliation is a restoration of the relationship. It works like this: When we forgive someone, we let go of the power of his hurtful actions or words over us. We acknowledge that it happened and that it hurt, and we call on God to help us let go of the power of that event. We don't need the other person's cooperation to do this; we only need our desire to forgive and our ability to call on God. That is it.

Reconciliation requires two people and God. Reconciliation starts when the other person asks our forgiveness. Reconciliation occurs if and when we recognize that the person who hurt us was acting out of character and will not attack our dignity again. This is big here. If someone asks our forgiveness, but continues to live and act in a way that is harmful to our human dignity, we must forgive him, but we cannot reconcile with him.

We have to remember this – each person has to protect her God-given human dignity. Any pattern of behavior that contradicts our knowledge that we are worth God's last breath is not something with which we can be reconciled. You are called, always and everywhere, to protect your human dignity.

Finally, we must remember that forgiveness is a process, not a moment. The first step in the process of forgiveness is the desire to forgive. It is quite possible to be so hurt by someone that we don't even want to forgive her. If this is the case, then we can pray for the desire to forgive. Either way, whether we have the desire to forgive, or are praying for the desire to forgive, we have started on the process of forgiveness.

The next step takes place in our daily prayer. Here, each day, we ask for the grace to forgive the person; to let go of the hurt and pain and to move on. We keep this up until we know we are free.

Along the way, it is good for us to keep two things in mind:

First, we don't have to pretend that we are not hurt. That is not forgiveness; that is lying. If someone hurt us, and we are trying to forgive her, then we don't have to pretend that we have already. Now, if we hurt someone and need his forgiveness, then we need to be sure and give him the space and time he needs to work through it himself.

Second, we need to be vigilant. Whenever we remember the pain or the moment that hurt us, we need to be strong and speak to it with the power of the Holy Spirit. For example, we can say "Jesus, help me to let go," or whatever we need to do in order to live free.

This process may take a long time; or it may not take nearly as long as we think. The important thing is not that we "complete this task," but that we are faithful in our efforts to try and forgive. Keep in mind that there will come a day when we recognize that, through God's grace, we have gotten stronger and are ready to move on.

Warning! Bad joke ahead!

A couple came into my office for some marriage prep meetings. I began talking about unconditional love and decided to give them a concrete example. I turned to the bride-to-be and said, "Now, suppose you two get married. One day your husband comes home and tells you that through gambling and bad investments, he's lost everything – no money, no credit cards, no savings, no checking account, nothing. Would you still love him?" She thought for a moment and said, "Yes, I would still love him, but I sure would miss him."

Chapter Three: Questions about relationships, emotions and values

Dear Fr. Joe,

I can't seem to get my grandson to go to church. His parents aren't taking him and I would really like him to go. What should I do?

I was at the grocery store the other day wearing my clerics and this guy came up and said, "You know, I don't go to church anymore because it's filled with hypocrites."

I said to him, "Don't worry, there is always room for one more!"

I hope he saw the truth in that statement. We all need church. I don't mean to be trite – the pain of a loved one not going to church is real, I know. When we talk about spiritual matters, we are often talking about people's souls and we want to take that seriously.

OK, so what do you do?

First of all, pray. This is not the "token" response: "Of course you say 'pray,' you're a priest!" No, this is the first and best course of action because it is the root of all we do.

Jesus spent time in prayer and we need to follow his example. This accomplishes numerous things. The two major aspects are that it helps us hand over the situation to Jesus and it takes the answer out of our hands so we are not prideful when God answers our prayers. Got it?

The second step is to have a chat with your grandson's parents. Show 'em this article if you want! (Hey, if you are the one reading this now, take your son to church! We need him!) Avoid condemnation or comments about their parenting skills. Just let them know how painful this situation is for you. Share in a personal way how faithful attendance at church has changed your life. Offer to drive them to church – do whatever it takes. This does not need to be about conflict; it can be a simple expression of your pain about this situation.

Now, let me take a moment to address all of you out there who have kids. First, PLEASE take your sons and daughters to church. As life gets more complicated and/or painful, their faith will be something they can always rely on. Don't let the spiritual legacy your parents built die with them. We don't let kids "make their own choices" about alcohol, drugs or sex, so let's make sure we don't wimp out on this one either.

Second, if you are taking your kids to church, make sure they know how important this is to you. Get to Mass on time and dress appropriately. Stay for the entire celebration. Explain how things work and why we do what we do.

Here is something you may not have thought about: Not only does your child need the church, the church needs your child! We are incomplete when all the baptized members of the church are not there. We need your daughter's or son's gifts and talents. They – and you – are important!

Finally, thank your own parents who took you to church. This is the best place for us to meet Jesus. This is what saves us and brings us closer to heaven. More often than not, our parents probably had to take some serious garbage from us to get us there. So thanks for taking it, Mom and Dad!

In my years as a priest, I have seen over and over how important a faith foundation is in life. Let's make sure we pass this on to the next generation.

Warning! Bad joke ahead!

One December night, my friend Fr. Mark went out to sing Christmas carols. When he went to the first house and began singing, an elderly man came to the door and tears began to roll down his face. Fr. Mark, seeing that the man was moved to tears, asked "Are you remembering happy childhood memories?" "No," the man sniffed, wiping a tear. "I'm a musician."

Dear Fr. Joe,

I'm in high school. How can I defend the Catholic faith? I'm not sure I know enough to argue with non-believers or non-Catholics, even though I know our faith stands for the truth.

As a Catholic young person, you'll find yourself defending the faith to two main types of people. The first type are atheists or agnostics. The second is made up of other Christians who do not accept Catholicism as Christianity. In this issue, we will deal with questions from atheists and agnostics.

The following are common questions that young people get asked, and it's not easy to answer them in a quick, easy format. Parents, I encourage you to work with your young people on these. Here we go!

How do we know there is a God?

Basically, I like to tackle this question from the angle of design. Look at it this way: If you come home on graduation day and find a huge sign at your front door that says "Congratulations, Graduate!" you automatically assume that someone made it for you. You don't marvel at the shocking confluence of random events that just happened to create a sign on your door that is addressed to you and your current situation; you assume that someone intentionally made it and put it there. It's the same with the world around you.

The basic idea is that whenever you and I see design, we assume someone designed it. We don't look at a painting and believe that a random explosion of paint and paper rendered a beautiful work of art; we assume that someone painted it.

The world we live in is infinitely more complicated than a painting. The interconnectedness of nature and the way our bodies work point to the work of a master creator. For someone to say that a random explosion created the world and all its intricacies requires a greater leap of faith than anything Catholicism asks of you.

Who created God? What was before God?

Wow, this one is tough, and it may hurt your hair trying to follow it, but stick with me – it's a great argument. Suppose I walk up to you and say "Did you change your oil?" and you respond, "Not recently. My car doesn't need it." Now, suppose I then said, "Not in your car, did you change your oil?" How would you respond?

In the end, I hope you would realize that the question does not apply to you. You don't have oil to change. The question doesn't even work.

It's the same with God. The terms "created" and "before" do not apply to God. Why do I say that? Well, we look at the world around us, how it works, and we realize a real basic, important truth: everything requires a cause. You are the perfect example of this. You did not materialize one day, you are the result of your parents creating you. Each of your parents are a result of their parents creating them, and on and on and on.

So, when and how does it start? Who were the first parents and how did they come into being? What was their cause? If you keep taking this backwards, you hit a brick wall.

If everything requires a cause, we see that nothing should have ever come to be! Creatures and creation that require a cause need to be created by something that doesn't need a cause. That which doesn't need a cause is what we call God.

God, by definition, is outside of time and uncreated. If God were inside of time and created, then he wouldn't be God. He would just be a really old dude.

Kick that one around and see if you can make it your own.

A lot of my information comes from Peter Kreeft's book, *Fundamentals of the Faith*. I highly recommend this book.

Warning! Bad joke ahead!

I was discussing the Ten Commandments with some of the fifth- and sixth-graders. After explaining the commandment to "Honor your father and mother," I asked, "Is there a commandment that teaches us how to treat our brothers and sisters?" Without missing a beat one little boy answered, "Thou shall not kill."

Dear Fr. Joe,
What does it mean to be pure in heart?

According to the philosopher Søren Kierkegaard, "To be pure in heart means to will one thing." I like that.

We do not want to limit purity to sexuality, though that is definitely an important element of it. We should think of purity of heart as pertaining to everything we do and all that we are.

What are you all about? What do you will? What do you desire? What do you want more than anything? The answers to these questions will tell us if we are pure in heart.

Our hearts need to be pure. When our hearts are pure, we will be who we were created to be. We desire nothing more than to be holy, righteous people who love Jesus above everything else.

Dear Fr. Joe,
In a world that corrupts the innocence of children so completely, what can I do to keep my child pure?

Wow – great question! In a world that doesn't even mention purity except when mocking it, it is essential that we be concerned with the purity of our children.

I am drawing my answer to this question from young people who write me from all over and the young people I have the honor and privilege of speaking to every day.

So, what can we do? I think it important that we tell them early on that our intention is to help them stay pure. Let your child know that you want this for them.

Early on, they need to learn that your family is different than most families out there. They should know that there will be things that their friends do that you will not allow them to do.

First, let's hit the don'ts:

Don't allow your child to drink with you. I think drinking with your child isn't "taking the mystery out of it." I think it's teaching them some horrible lessons; that they need alcohol to relax and have a good time, and that you believe the rules (i.e., laws) don't apply to you and your family.

Another challenge to purity is allowing teens to travel together. Going on trips with their girlfriends or boyfriends is not a good way to monitor their behavior. It's putting them into a situation that is way too tempting for them to generally handle. They need to learn that dating is not a recreational activity. There are people's hearts involved, and we don't recreate with those.

Letting your child "get it out of his/her system" is not a recommended excuse for sinful behavior. I fall back on one of my old redneck sayings here: "If you want a wild dog off your porch, don't feed it." Sin works the same way. We don't feed it to get rid of it.

Monitor the TV. This one is huge. As a general rule, television sends your kids a message that is radically contrary to the Gospel.

Don't be your child's friend. They have enough of those. Be their parent. Do not hesitate to tell them what is right and wrong and enforce discipline. Young people know when authority is "all talk."

Now, let's cover the dos:

Take your child to church. Early on, young people need to see the value of faithfulness. Faithfulness to God is essential to their spiritual and emotional development. They should know that no matter what happens, they are going to church. Even if they fight you, give them that one thing they can count on always happening.

Pray with your child. Not just before meals, but every day as a family. My folks never let social, athletic or extracurricular activities interfere with the daily ritual of sitting down together after dinner to take time to pray.

Show your child love and affection. Let them know they are God's gift to you and more important than anything else. Don't assume they know you love them. Teenagers in particular tend to struggle with feeling loved.

Dear Fr. Joe,
When does sharing information become gossip?

Such a great, practical question! I think there is a fine line here and crossing it is easier than we think. Let me give you two basic rules and let's see if that helps.

Rule No. 1: If someone approaches you with some information, or if you are ready to share some, ask yourself the question, "Why am I sharing this?" Or ask the person talking, "Why are you telling me this?" If the answer is anything other than life-giving and helpful, then you are engaging in gossip. That question is so powerful that it knocks the darkness into the light and anything that shouldn't be there is exposed for the sin it is. Try this one – it can really hurt. The good kind of hurt, that is.

Rule No. 2: "Venting" is a term we have come up with to justify gossip. If our answer to the question, "Why are you telling me this?" is "venting," then we probably have gossiped. I would like to see us adopt the mind-set that we would rather suffer from holding something in than risk gossiping and hurting another. Obviously, spouses are excluded from this rule, since openly communicating your feelings with your spouse is a way to learn, grow, forgive and gain understanding.

Dear Fr. Joe,
When should you confront someone with the truth?

What's with all the tough questions?

Let's begin with the premise that we often hesitate to speak the truth for two reasons. One, because we are afraid of hurting someone and, two, because we are afraid of being hypocritical.

Let's look at the idea that we are afraid of hurting someone. Look at this quote from Pope Benedict XVI: "Ultimately, the truth is pastoral."

What does that mean? Look at *John 14:6*. In it, Jesus says, "I am the way, the truth and the life." Remember, truth is a person, Jesus Christ, so we treat the truth with reverence and respect. When we slander someone, or use the truth to gain power for ourselves, we have violated the commandment against taking God's name in vain.

So, when you and I speak the truth in love, we are invoking Jesus. We always want to make sure that we speak the truth in a way that honors God.

What about being hypocritical? Remember this – if we were allowed only to speak on what we "have down," then we would never speak. We are hypocrites, not when we speak against behavior that we engage in and don't like, but when we speak as if we don't have the same problems. A hypocrite is someone who pretends he or she has it "together" and speaks in order to further that myth.

Let's not wait until people's pattern of behavior is so destructive that they are at death's door or at the bottom of the barrel. Let's speak the truth in love when it will help them and elevate them. Let's purify our hearts and motives and always be ready to live in the truth.

Warning! Bad joke ahead!

A surgery professor died and went to heaven. At the pearly gates, he was asked by the gatekeeper, "Have you ever committed a sin you truly regret?" "Yes," the professor answered. "When I was an intern at Saint Lucas Hospital, we played soccer against the Community Hospital team, and I scored the winning goal. The referee didn't see that it was off-side and I didn't tell him. I regret that now."

"Well," said the gatekeeper. "That is a very minor sin. Come in."

"Thank you, Saint Peter," the professor answered.

"Oh, I'm not Saint Peter," said the gatekeeper. "He's at lunch. I'm Saint Lucas."

Dear Fr. Joe,
I keep quiet about things going on in my life because everything I say gets spread around. What should I do?

This is a tough one. As a general rule, we seem to be losing our sense of honor as a society. We are way too quick to spread what we hear. As I said earlier, the term "venting" is usually our excuse to break a confidence.

What should you do? Well, your options are limited here because we cannot control other people. The only thing you can control in your life is what you share, not what people do with it, so let's take a look at what you share.

Think of it like this – everything about you is a treasure. God made you in his own image and likeness. The thoughts of your mind and the feelings of your heart – all of these things are precious treasures that are God's gift to you and your gift to God. Be careful with these treasures. Treat them gently. Don't share them with people who are not trustworthy.

Try to remember that great bit of secular advice – "Fool me once, shame on you. Fool me twice, shame on me."

Now, on the other side of the coin, remember that a treasure locked up in a closet is no good to anyone – this is why we display artwork in museums. When you or I share some of the treasure that is ourselves with other people, they are elevated. They are made more whole, because you have shared God's gift with them.

So what do you do? Share your heart and mind only with people who are trustworthy. The right people will come along soon; just hang in there.

Warning! Bad joke ahead!

All the monks in a certain monastery sing the simple word "Morning!" from their windows each sunrise. Early one day after several "Morning!" greetings have been sung melodiously into the dawn air, a single greeting of "Evening!" rings out of one window. In the courtyard below, Brother Timothy looks around startled, and chants in a single note, "Did you hear that, Brother Edward?" "Hear what, Brother Timothy?" replied Brother Edward in an echoed chant. Brother Timothy sang: "Someone chanted evening ..." Groan.

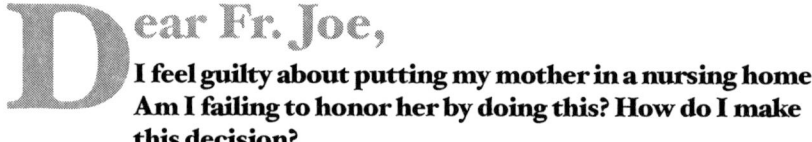

Dear Fr. Joe,

I feel guilty about putting my mother in a nursing home. Am I failing to honor her by doing this? How do I make this decision?

This is a tough one, and the fact that it is a difficult decision for you is a good sign that you want to respect and honor your mother. I often remember the words of St. Francis DeSales, who says that the desire to love God is, in fact, loving God. In the same way, your desire to honor your mother is probably your first sign that you are doing so.

Often times, though, our desire to do well bumps into the practicalities of living in "the real world." So, how do we know the right thing to do?

As is our custom as Catholics, let's jump right into the ***catechism***. This is a rather long quote, but well worth reading:

The family should live in such a way that its members learn to care and take responsibility for the young, the old, the sick, the handicapped and the poor. There are many families who are at times incapable of providing this help. It devolves then on the other persons, other families, and, in a subsidiary way, society to provide for their needs: *"Religion that is pure and undefiled before God and the Father is this: to visit orphans and widows in their affliction and to keep oneself unstained from the world." (CCC 2208, cf. Jas 1:27)*

Let's take that apart. First of all, in the church's mind, it seems that before this decision is made, a lifestyle must be lived that teaches children in the home that it is our duty to care for those who are incapable or limited in their ability to care for themselves. This is an important idea and, hopefully, a challenge to parents to take time out of their own busy schedules to teach their children through example and practice how to care for others. Readers, when is the last time we took our children to a soup kitchen? When is the last time we brought food to a homeless shelter? When is the last time we delivered Double Stuf Oreos® to priests who write for magazines? (Where did that come from?) Hopefully, this type of behavior lays a foundation for our young people to see that caring for others is a top priority for a Catholic family.

Once we have done that, then our extremely difficult decision to place a loved one in a nursing home is an expression of an attitude that we have shown our children over and over throughout their lives: sometimes, our support and honor of the dignity of the human person translates into placing them with those who can care for them best. In this day and age, when people are living longer, this seems to happen more often.

So, in the end, it seems to me that there will be times when our ability to care for someone we love is not equal to the care they need. When that happens, it may be time to place them in a nursing home that will give them the love and care they need. However, when that happens, our responsibilities do not end.

Truth be told, I have been to many nursing homes in my day. I have seen the best possible scenarios and some pretty bad ones, as well. What makes the ultimate difference for those who must live there? It is not always the way the nursing home is run. Instead, the experience is usually positive or negative based on whether or not the family comes to visit. Moms, dads, brothers, sisters, grandchildren, nephews and nieces – all of them – should inundate residents with love and affection. Remind them of their importance as human beings. Thank them for their contributions to our lives. Ask about those stories they are so famous for. Play cards, checkers, everything. Once the decision is made to place a loved one in nursing home care, we must constantly pester those who love them with requests to visit.

Even then, our responsibilities do not end. We must next move outside of our family life and look at the life of our country. Politically, we are called to care for the elderly as well. All of this ties into the "seamless garment" of the "culture of life" that our Holy Father speaks about. We must be politically aware of those who will seek to make life better for those who struggle in society. We must truly be "pro-life" in our voting and support – or non-support! – of political candidates. In my mind, it begins with supporting those who protect and defend life from the moment of conception until natural death – which includes everything in between. By the way, a candidate who wants to throw money at a problem is not necessarily acting in the best interests of those who have the problem.

Finally, let's all remember to pray for those who are alone, sick, alienated and in need of help. This is always the first and best course of action.

Warning! Bad joke ahead!

I was at a social event and I met a really nice couple. We were chatting away, getting to know each other and everything was going well when one of them asked me, "Hey, what do you think of clown ministry?" It has always been a habit of mine to show restraint and forethought whenever I speak (Dad, Mom, quit laughing!), so I launched into a speech saying how much I couldn't stand clown ministry, clowns scared me ever since I was a kid, blah, blah, blah. I went on and on speaking about my dislike for clowns for a good five minutes when I noticed them looking at me strangely. After a good two-minute pause, the husband looked at me and said, "We were just asking because we have a clown ministry."

Someday, somehow, I will learn to shut my mouth ...

Dear Fr. Joe,

One of my brothers says he is no longer Catholic. He and his wife seem to spend a great deal of time criticizing my family and the Catholic Church. He says we aren't going to heaven. It's really hard at family gatherings because he is always trying to convert people. What should I do?

Wow! Questions like this are tough. Obviously, your brother has had a powerful religious experience and wants to share it. That's a good thing. The bad thing is that he is not accepting your religious experience.

So, here is what we do.

First of all, he is probably asking you if you have a personal relationship with Jesus Christ. That is something you need to be able to answer. The sacraments offer us the chance to have this relationship, but we have to respond by saying "yes" to Jesus every day and seeking to love God and his people every chance we get. If that is true in your life, let him know! Tell him, "Yes, I love Jesus, and I share it in word and deed!" If it is not true, then work on it. Get to know Jesus through some quiet time and reading of the Scriptures. Go to Mass and receive the Eucharist. Let Jesus be your savior.

OK, so we've covered that.

It also may be that your brother needs someone to listen to him. It does seem in our culture that it is OK to talk to anybody about anything – as long as it isn't about Jesus. Maybe your brother is expressing an appropriate desire but in an inappropriate way – he wants to talk about faith! Share with him and let him share with you!

Now, all of this is assuming that your brother and his spouse will accept your faith in Jesus through the Catholic Church as authentic. This is a big assumption and, to be honest, about 90 percent of the time, they won't treat your beliefs with any respect at all.

So, what then?

Has it occurred to you that you have nothing to apologize for in being Catholic? I am always amazed at the low opinion other Christian churches have of us and how often that opinion is born of ignorance. Get to know this faith you love so much and you will be able to share your Catholicism as well. There are great Web resources to do this in the back of this book.

Or it could be that your brother and his wife don't want to share – they only want to yell at you. If this is the case, be as patient as you can (there are worse things – he could be selling magazine subscriptions during dinner) and pray for them. Prayer is a powerful tool.

It may be that your prayers and the acceptance you offer them is all they need to "love God without embarrassing Jesus" as Tony Campolo says. A couple of last tactical points for discussing your faith in a hostile environment include your **catechism**, which is an outstanding resource. Be sure and look up the different topics you are challenged on. If a Scripture is quoted to you, ask for chapter and verse so you can look it up yourself. Finally, remember the words of St. Augustine: "In essential things, unity. In the inessentials, liberty. In all things, love."

I read a great story from Billy Graham. He tells of a time early in his ministry when he arrived in a small town to preach a sermon. Wanting to mail a letter, he asked a young boy where the post office was. When the boy told him, Dr. Graham thanked him and said, "If you'll come to the church this evening, you can hear me telling everyone how to get to heaven." "I don't think I'll be there," the boy said. "You don't even know your way to the post office."

Dear Fr. Joe,

I am quite angry at some people at our parish over decisions they have made in our church. I am angry and I am hurt. What should I do?

Conflict stinks, doesn't it? It is hard to learn to live together in peace when we keep stepping on each other's toes! An early saint once said, "Community life is penance enough for anyone."

So, what do we do when two Christians disagree? Here are some rules that I have found helpful. First of all, we have to pray. I know, I know! I say that every time but it is a message in and of itself, right?

Second, we have to go to the person who offended us. This is a must. Spreading talk about our anger is gossip, pure and simple. We can do great damage to someone's reputation when we do that. Nobody likes to be talked about and we have to keep that in mind. Also, we need to do this face to face. Writing an anonymous letter is not only counterproductive, it is cowardly.

When we go to that person (or persons), we must make sure we love them. Confronting someone we hate produces more anger – it doesn't relieve it. So, even if we don't feel love, we must remember our commitment to love.

If anyone says, "I love God," but hates his brother, he is a liar; for whoever does not love a brother whom he has seen cannot love God whom he has not seen. **(1 Jn 4:20)**

Ouch! I don't mean love as an emotion, but as a commitment on our part to see the person we disagree with as someone who Jesus died for and loves very much.

Third, we have to assume the best. This means we assume their intent was to do the right thing – they love God as much as we do and are seeking holiness with purity of heart.

Fourth, we have to keep in mind that our perceptions may be wrong and we have to be willing to accept that.

I know all these steps are easy to write but hard to do. However, we are called to nothing less. How we disagree with someone can be a witness to the world about the power and value of Christianity. AND, in each of these steps we have to pray, pray, pray! We are incapable of acting this way through our own strength – it requires grace. Read and reflect on ***Matthew 18***.

Warning! Bad joke ahead!

Is anyone else confused by the new, trendy signs used in restaurants to designate men's and women's bathrooms? Recently, at a local establishment, I wandered off in search of the men's room and found myself looking at two doors – one marked "The Dunes" and the other "The Oasis." I grabbed an employee who was walking by and told him I needed to use the bathroom. Pointing at the doors, I asked, "Which one should I use?" "Actually, we would prefer you to go there," the employee said, pointing to a door down the hall marked "MEN." "The Dunes and Oasis are private dining rooms."

Dear Fr. Joe,

My parents are trying to stop me from hanging out with some friends from school. I think they are judging them without getting to know them. What do you think?

I like this question and I'm glad you asked. The first thing we have to look at is the issue of obedience. Obedience is not a word that is used often in our day and age, but it is an important one. As young people living at home, it is important to learn the value of obedience. Obedience is an acceptance on our part that there are people out there who know more than us. It is nothing less than our call as Christians.

As an adult who is a priest, I work hard at obedience. It is a skill that we all need to succeed in life and grow in love of Jesus and His Bride, the church. Remember, it is Jesus' obedience that saved us.

So, why would your parents ask you to be obedient on this matter? Probably because your mother and/or father are judging. And that is not a bad thing. For example, I love Little Debbie® Snack Cakes. I mean, I REALLY love Little Debbie® Snack Cakes. If there was a religion based around Little Debbie® Snack Cakes, I would … well, you get the point. Now, if I were to eat them as often as I wanted, the results would eventually be disastrous. I would probably end up the size of a small Eastern European country right before I died of a massive heart attack.

How do I know this? Have I ever gone through a period in my life where I ate nothing but Little Debbie® Snack Cakes, resulting in significant weight gain and eventual death? No, I am making a judgment – a judgment based on doctors' wisdom and other people's life experiences.

You see where I am going? Your parents have a significant amount of life experience. They have seen things. They know what to look for.

Another example: Do you have younger brothers and/or sisters? Think of what you know that they don't. Remember how they used to want to touch the cool-looking, glowing red thing in the kitchen? You saw a cool-looking, glowing red thing there, too, but you knew that touching it would result in a burned hand. So, you kept your little brother or sister from it – even if it made them angry.

In the same way, your parents are trying to protect you and they are willing to risk losing your affection to save you from unnecessary pain. This is what heroes do and this is what makes parents so wonderful.

Now, you might be saying, "Jesus said never to judge." No, Jesus said not to judge or we risk being judged. But being judged is not a bad thing if we live our lives in accordance with God's commands. Also, Jesus gave commands to his followers to do things that were very judgmental. He told his disciples to leave towns that reject the message and "shake the dust off your feet in testament against them." *(Mk 6:11)* There are Scripture passages where Jesus called people a "brood of vipers" *(Mt 12:34)* and "whitewashed tombs, which appear beautiful on the outside, but inside are full of dead men's bones and every kind of filth." *(Mt 23:27)* How does that jibe with "stop judging, that you may not be judged?" *(Mt 7:1)*

Jesus was talking about motivation. We cannot judge other people's motives. These people you want to hang out with may have great motivation, but live it out in a way that is destructive.

Check this last point out. It's a little tough, but I think it is valuable, too. When I was in Israel, I heard an incredible comment on Christian art. You know the picture where Jesus is a shepherd and he is carrying a small lamb on his shoulders? I used to look at that picture and think it was sweet.

Then I found out the truth.

If you ever see a shepherd carrying a small lamb like that, it's because the lamb's leg is broken. Sounds reasonable, right?

Well, here is the thing – the lamb's leg is broken because the shepherd broke it. I found out that if a shepherd has a sheep that will not stay with the group and tends to wander around, he'll break its leg and carry it around until the leg heals. This is for two reasons. First because "a sheep that wanders is a sheep that is dead." Sheep are so helpless they won't last a day away from the protection of the shepherd or the safety of the group. Second, once that lamb's leg heals, it will not leave the shepherd's side – ever.

It's a tough story, gruesome even, but an important point. Hanging out with the wrong people will hurt us and bring us pain. It might be great at first, but it will ultimately destroy us and hurt people around us. Like the shepherd, our parents may have to make some tough choices, even forbidding us to hang out with certain people, but they are doing this to save us – to keep us from pain that is not necessary.

I want to wrap this up with a story from my own experience. I am blessed with two really great friends. These two guys are the best friends I've got

Chapter Three: Questions about relationships, emotions and values

– they bring out the best in me and I try to bring out the best in them. They understand my schedule; they walk with me when things are tough; and, let me walk with them when they need it. That's good stuff, but so is this – they give me the business when I need that as well. "How's your prayer life, Joe?" "Joe, you really shouldn't have done that." "You need to slow down." Comments like this are uncomfortable for them to say and hard for me to receive, but they care more about my salvation and betterment as a human than their own comfort. This is a strength to me, and I rely on them heavily.

But this is what friends do. They don't just hang out with us and support everything we do. They question us when we need it and challenge us to do and be better.

The ultimate challenge? Real friends risk losing our friendship in order to save our souls or help us to improve as human beings. THAT is the good stuff. That is what a friend does.

Just like Jesus did.

Dear Fr. Joe,
I caught my boyfriend talking to his old girlfriend. I'm really jealous. I know this isn't a good thing, but how do I handle it?

It's funny, but on this one, I gotta start with the key I always start with: prayer.

See, as I write this article, I am on my laptop in front of the Blessed Sacrament. I am asking Jesus to help me communicate his love and truth to you through me. This is a big task; by asking this question you are putting a lot of trust in me and I have the responsibility to lead you the right way as best I can.

So, what do I do? I pray. So should you.

All of us, because of our past, because of our experiences of living in a fallen world, have different things that we struggle with. These struggles are opportunities for us to call on God and ask for divine assistance. We all hit roadblocks in life; some of them are because of our sins, some of them are because of others.

I can't speak as to whether or not you should trust your boyfriend; I do not know him or you well enough, but here is what I do know: You can only control you, and the best way for you to do that is to pray for God to give you wisdom in this situation and to help you see if he is worthy of trust.

If he is worthy of trust, then ask God to help you grow here. Make sure and ask your parents to pray with you and challenge you to be more trusting. If he is not, then for the sake of your own dignity, you need to walk away. You are worth the best God has to offer; accept nothing less.

Warning! Bad joke ahead!

My nephew is an optimist or a saint. I am not sure which yet; I will have to let you know. The reason I type this is because of something that happened at church the other day. The Mass was just beginning and the priest invited the congregation to take a moment and call upon their sins. As soon as the priest finished speaking, my nephew piped up and in a loud voice said, "I'm done!"

Dear Fr. Joe,
My boyfriend won't let me talk to my friends anymore and wants me to quit activities he's not in. Is this normal?

No that's not normal, nor healthy. Here is the deal; each and every one of us is a treasure. We are created in the image and likeness of God. That makes us special, unique – a treasure. Your gifts, your talents, your personality – the whole you is created as God's gift to the world. But we are a treasure that is meant to be shared.

Now, seeing what is great about you is easy, because you are amazing. But we have to take the next step: Anyone who truly loves you does not only see and love what is beautiful about you, but they want others to see and honor that beauty.

Here is another thing to think about: Pope John Paul II said that we were created because of love and we are created for love. He was not speaking of an emotion – he was speaking of love as a state of being. You see, love is a concept that takes us an eternity to learn; that is why heaven is forever. As you travel on in life, you will learn more and more about love, and hopefully, this young man will as well.

But, what you and he must learn is that some key components of love are freedom and trust. Since I explored trust in the last question, I am going to focus on freedom.

What does freedom mean in regard to love? Well, quite simply, that true love sets us free. Do you feel free in this relationship? Does thinking about it elevate you and encourage you to grow? I can't imagine that is the case. So what does that mean?

In terms of your boyfriend, I will be blunt; you need to get out and get out quick. The actions you describe are not the actions of a healthy person, nor are they the actions of someone who loves you.

Pray for God to give you the strength to do the right thing, make absolutely sure you talk to your folks about this and get their input and support.

I will pray for you as well.

Dear Fr. Joe,
What do I do if a friend is suicidal?

One of the students at the Catholic high school where I serve as chaplain committed suicide. It was one of the most difficult times I have experienced in all my years at the school. I am writing this column about suicide in response to a question mailed to me. The answer comes from being a part of the slow and painful healing process that everyone goes through when someone chooses to take his or her life. Please pray today that all of us will grow in our ability to know our value in the eyes of God. May Jesus bless you today.

Tough times, obviously – you have my prayers.

Now, what do you do?

First of all, you have to recognize that you are in an important position as a friend. If you know your friend is suicidal, then one of two things is true: One possibility is that your friend told you that he is thinking of suicide. If that is the case, then that means your friend has trusted you with his secret. You have earned something great because of the way you care, and that speaks very well of you. The second possibility is that you have watched your friend and picked up on subtle signs that something is amiss, and that you see the possibility of her hurting herself. If that is the case, this also speaks well of you; you are an observant, sensitive person who is aware of your friends at a time in your life when it is hard not to be self-focused. I am telling you these things because you need to keep them in your heart, as things are about to get rough.

The first step is to be sure that you are talking with your friend about his or her feelings; "How are you doing today? Is there anything I can do?" Questions like this are an invitation to take what is hidden in the darkness and bring them out into the light. They are more than questions; they are a statement of care and concern. As your friend shares his heart with you, make sure that you are really listening. Find out what is going on and what you can do to help. Often, the best thing you can do to help is to be available and offer him all your love and prayers.

Now, if in your conversations, you realize that she is serious about taking her own life, you need to be sure and be present to her as much as you can. Get a group of trusted people to stay close while you take the next step, which is the difficult one.

See, the next step is that you need to take this to an adult. The hardest part here will be your feelings of guilt about breaking a confidence. It could also be that you are thinking "Well, I could be wrong and if I am, I'll really embarrass my friend."

I think it's worth it, don't you? Suicide is a permanent condition. There are no second chances in a situation like this. It is much better to make an error on the side of caution than to be at a funeral and wonder what you could have done.

With that in your heart and mind, then, be sure and talk to a trusted adult; a good option would seem to be your friend's parents, assuming they are not part of the problem. If you can't talk to them, you may want to talk to your own parents. In fact, you may want to talk to your parents first. Sometimes, they may have suggestions about whom you should be telling about this situation. There is also the possibility of talking to one of your teachers, or the counselor at school. There are so many people you can go to in a situation like this — make sure you take this step!

Now, if the person is threatening to kill himself at that moment, don't hesitate – pick up the phone and call 9-1-1. Don't worry about "wasting their time." I assure you, the numerous police officers I have talked to on this issue would rather respond to a call to prevent a teen suicide than a call to report one.

Some people will tell you, "Well, she's only doing it to get attention," and that may very well be the case. However, if she is only "doing it to get attention," then she must need attention pretty badly, because talking about killing yourself is a pretty drastic step. Don't use the possibility of "attention-getting" as a reason to step away, let it compel you even more to get involved. Any time a person threatens to kill herself, or says he wants to be dead, you should take it very seriously.

If you are reading this and struggling with suicidal thoughts yourself, make sure you talk to someone who can help: your parents, your priest or teacher, a friend; anyone who can help.

Life is a precious, beautiful gift — we all need to take care of and cherish that gift the best we can.

Chapter Three: Questions about relationships, emotions and values

Warning! Bad joke ahead!

So, I'm driving through a local neighborhood when I see a young boy with a lemonade stand. The sign says "All you can drink – 55 cents." Now, being a firm believer in supporting local businesses (as well as being thirsty), I decided this was a good deal. I paid my 55 cents and was given a little paper cup of lemonade. I drank it down and asked for another when the boy said, "Sure, you can have another for 55 cents." I confess to being a bit shocked and pointed to the sign. The young man responded, "Right. That's all you can drink for 55 cents."

Dear Fr. Joe,
My brother has totally distanced himself from our parents. He keeps in touch with a couple of siblings, but his behavior toward our folks has created tension in our large family. How can we handle this without getting in the middle of a family meltdown?

Such a tough issue; families are such a source of strength and love, and can also be the source of our biggest struggles and pains. I've done a shocking amount of family counseling and believe I have some wisdom to offer you.

The first thing to remember is that family bonds are sacred. The first commandment with a promise is the fourth and it concerns family. There are numerous Scriptures and documents on the power and beauty of family and we need to keep that knowledge in our hearts.

With these ideas in mind, I'd like to share with you some of my "Family Commandments." Ready?

We must not take each other for granted. This one is easy to mess up. Because we see each other every day and know each other so intimately, it is quite possible for us to forget how beautiful our parents and brothers and sisters are. The key here in my mind is gratitude. We simply must, at least once a week, take some time and think of each member of our family and why we are grateful for them. For my part, I often remind my family of how grateful they should be for me. Did I mention that I do that often?

We must forgive. If we don't forgive each other for our failings, we will become unpleasant people in every aspect of our lives. Because of our emotional and physical proximity, it is inevitable that we will be hurt by each other. We must remember to forgive each other's failings and ask forgiveness for ours. My dad and mom never allowed us to say, "I'm sorry" and leave it there. We had to ask each other's forgiveness; they didn't just teach us that, they modeled it.

We must respect. The word "respect" comes from two words in Latin that we stuck together: *re,* which means "again" and *spect,* which is the root of the words spectator and spectacle – it means "to look at." So, when I state that we need to respect everyone in our family, that means we must look at them again and see who they really are and what their place in our life needs to be. For example, if you look at your youngest brother again, he may just need Double Stuf Oreos.® It could be that simple.

We must not hold anyone in our family to a standard we can't keep. This one is huge. Before you complain about your parents' failures or how your siblings don't measure up, perhaps it is time, in the words of Jesus, to "remove the wooden beam from your eye first." *(Mt 7:5)* I have news for you: you weren't a perfect parent – or a perfect brother, sister, or child. You were a mess some days. Your family still loved you as best they could and I'm thinking that is something you should imitate.

There are no positive side effects of gossip. That call to "vent" or "get his opinion"? Yeah. That's gossip, and it didn't help. If you can't talk to the person who offended you or who didn't act properly, then you can't talk about it. It's that simple.

Jesus first. You know why clichés stick around, even though everyone hates them? Because often, they communicate an essential truth. Brace now for the cliché: The family that prays together stays together.

There it is. I typed it. It's good stuff, though, folks; no amount of human love or wisdom will suffice, you have to put Jesus first and ask him to be your guide and your strength so that your love and wisdom come from God.

Now, what about your brother? Hopefully, this is helping you to see what you need to do: you need to pray that God guide your words and actions and then allow God to use you as he sees fit. Maybe you are going to be the one who builds the bridge, maybe you will be the one who draws the line in the sand…who knows? Remember the words of Jesus in Matthew that no amount of worry will help and then, anytime you do fret about this, make sure and pray and dedicate it to Jesus.

Between that and the "Family Commandments," I believe great and beautiful things are in store for your family.

Chapter Three: Questions about relationships, emotions and values

Dear Fr. Joe,

I'm a woman in my late 30s. The chances of me getting married at this point appear to be slim and none. I'm sick of people asking me why I'm not married – it doesn't seem to occur to them that I would be if I'd fallen in love and someone had asked me! I'm already struggling with the fact that God hasn't seen fit to send me someone to spend my life with.

Isn't it odd that the same society that makes marriage so easily dissolvable treats unmarried people like there is something wrong with them? Sigh.

It's been a long time, but I remember when I was in high school, we read books in our religious education by a woman named Lee Ezell. She wrote and spoke about topics of love, marriage and dating in a way that really made a lot of sense. I remember one thing she said in particular: "If you are not happy and complete as a single person, you will never be happy and complete as a married person." Or, as a dear friend of mine said, "I would rather wake up alone in the middle of the night then wake up with someone alone in the middle of the night."

Marriage doesn't complete anyone, Jesus does. People who are so rude as to inquire or comment on your status in life, be it married or single, need to be told they are being rude. May I suggest the line, "I'm curious as to what makes you think that is an appropriate question?"

Let's get back to you here.

I would imagine it's painful for you right now when you think about your lack of a husband; whatever the truth about us, we are physical creatures and the absence of a person we can see and touch in our lives who tells us we are loved can be extremely difficult. I believe it was, of all people, Sartre who said that at times, the biggest presence in our lives can be an absence.

I love being a priest more than anything in the world and I honestly can't believe God lets me do this, but even with that, there are times where I see all my nephews and nieces and experience that sadness that comes when I realize I will not have children of my own. This doesn't mean I don't love the priesthood or that I don't love my life; it just means that I'm a human experiencing human emotion.

The fact is, we can know the truth about God and ourselves and still feel pain; that's not a failure on our part – that's reality.

So, what do we do in those times of sorrow? I think these simple steps can offer some comfort.

First, (surprise!) pray. Ask God to walk with you in your sadness. Bring who you are and what you feel to Jesus and lay it at his feet. The Scriptures remind us often that "the Lord is close to the brokenhearted." *(Ps 34:19)*

Second, remind yourself of the truth. The fact is, marriage does not make you complete; only a personal encounter with the risen Jesus can do that. When we encounter Jesus, we can know his love. When we know Jesus' love, there is a sense of completeness that comes with that moment. Let's take a look at your value: Through his actions, God shows that you are worth all his blood and all his breath. He offers himself to you in the Eucharist and reconciles any brokenness in your relationship with him through the sacrament of reconciliation. You are unique in creation; capable of choosing to accept or reject God's love. This is what defines you more than anything else. In light of the fact that you are loved perfectly by the author of love, what else compares?

Third, focus on others is always a great way to draw attention away from our hurt. There are so many people with so many needs out there and God is calling you to enter into that world of need and be his presence. Be it the soup kitchen or various parish committees or commissions, there are so many ways that God can use you. I find that in helping others, I often forget my own struggles.

Finally, trust in God. If you place your future in God's hands then you can trust that God will get you where you need to be. St. Francis DeSales reminds us that if we ask God to guide us and stay open to the promptings of the Spirit, we can always be sure that we are where God wants us.

Warning! Bad joke ahead!

One time at seminary, we were going through the lunch line. At the head of the table was a large pile of apples. Someone had made a note and posted it on the tray of apples. The note said, "Take only ONE. God is watching." Moving further along the lunch line, at the other end of the table was a large pile of chocolate chip cookies. On that pile was a note written in a different hand that stated, "Take all you want. God is watching the apples."

Chapter Three: Questions about relationships, emotions and values

Chapter 4
Questions about issues of the day

A country lady, who has been taken to her first show at an art gallery in the big city, is staring curiously at several of the paintings. One is a huge canvas that is black with yellow blobs of paint splattered all over it. The next painting is a murky gray color that has drips of purple paint streaked across it. The country lady, filled with curiosity over the unusual works of art, walks over to the artist and says, "I don't understand your paintings. Could you tell me about them?"

"I paint what I feel inside me," shrugs the artist.

"Have you ever tried Alka-Seltzer?"

Dear Fr. Joe,
What's so bad about being gay? What about gay marriage? I know some gay couples who are more committed to healthy, lifelong relationships than many heterosexual couples. Isn't there some hypocrisy in the church on this issue?

This is a really sensitive topic. As Catholics, we have a stand on homosexuality that many interpret badly, or even use to justify hatred.

Before we get into the teaching itself, I think it important to remind ourselves of something: It's possible to disagree with someone and love them. I travel and lecture a bit and am discovering more and more that Americans are becoming incapable of separating an opinion or belief from their own selves. As Christians, it is our duty to speak the truth in love, but when the truth involves telling people we don't agree with their lifestyle or actions, we have to demonstrate to them the premise, "I can disagree with you and love you."

With that as a background, let's break it down, shall we? The church breaks its teaching into three sections:

1. Homosexual activity is intrinsically disordered.

2. Individuals with homosexual attractions are called to celibacy.

3. Discrimination or hostility against homosexual persons is a serious sin.

Let's take these one step at a time.

No. 1 is covered in **section 2357 of the catechism**. In it, the church teaches that homosexual activity is contrary to the natural law and that it closes off the sexual act to the gift of life. The section ends with this statement: "Under no circumstances can [homosexual acts] be approved." The scriptural backings for this come from ***Genesis 19:1-29, Romans 1:24-27, I Corinthians 6:9-10, and I Timothy 1:10***.

No. 2 is covered in **sections 2358 and 2359 of our catechism**. In these sections, the church makes it clear that if a homosexual person is Christian, they are to accept this suffering in the same way that Jesus accepted his sufferings; to "unite to the sacrifice of the Lord's cross the difficulties they may encounter from their condition." Also, through sacramental grace and prayer, homosexual persons are called to approach "Christian perfection" in the same way that all are called.

No. 3 is covered in **section 2358**. In it, the church reminds us that all homosexual persons are to be treated with respect, compassion and sensitivity. Their human dignity is the same as everyone else's, and "every sign of unjust discrimination in their regard should be avoided."

This is the core of the church's teaching on homosexuality.

Now, based on experience of talking about these ideas with my students, allow me to clarify a few points:

First of all, we are not talking here about "who goes to hell." Please, purge your minds and hearts of the need to figure out or speak authoritatively on who is in hell; it's usurping God's authority to pretend we can speak definitively on these things. I'm learning that high-schoolers in particular have trouble with this: When we say, "That action is wrong," they tend to go home and say, "Our teacher said gay people go to hell." Parents, please explain this to your children well.

Second, let's make sure that our theology is never an excuse to hate people. The church can and should lead the way in working with our brothers and sisters in the gay community to show the kind of love Jesus did.

As a society, we must learn the vast difference between acceptance and tolerance. In this case, we define acceptance as saying that something is

Chapter Four: Questions about issues of the day

good/moral, where tolerance is saying the person is sacred and loved by God, but their behavior is something we disagree with. John Paul II explained this concept at length in his writings, calling us to speak the truth in love and walk with people in their hurt.

Let's pray for the grace to be so loving and kind in our actions that we actually win people over to the message of Jesus.

Dear Fr. Joe,
Do you give to the panhandler? I feel guilty walking by someone, but I'm afraid giving money just perpetuates the problem.

There are, in my mind, a few ways people respond to beggars. One school of thought says that if you give them anything, you are participating in sin, because they may be taking that money and doing something evil or unhealthy with it.

I'm not a big fan of this school of thought. The people who say it probably pay taxes – and you know that not all the money our government collects is used for life-giving, wholesome things. Not giving people money because they might do something evil with it is – in my mind – usually a justification for a lack of charity, or revelatory of an unhealthy distrust of people.

The second school of thought starts off on a similar vein, but ends with a holy twist: Don't give beggars money when they ask, but be sure and buy them something to eat. I like this idea. Ignoring a beggar or instructing him about getting his life together does not work and is not helpful. However, choosing to feed a hungry person or get her a place for the night? Wow – that is good stuff! In fact, it is one of the reasons you and I are put on the earth. (One of the other reasons is tied intricately to Double Stuf Oreo® consumption, but I won't go into that here.) The great thing about this response is that it offers help, reminds the beggar of his value and worth, and reminds the giver of what she is called to do, all while minimizing the risk of your help being misused.

The third school of thought says that whenever you are approached, you help in any way you can. I like this as well. I have given money to panhandlers with a strong sense that they were going to use it to buy alcohol, but I didn't have the time or resources to go buy them food. I guess that, in the end, I would rather be burned for being naive than for being cynical.

The key is to respond! Homeless people often speak of being perceived as "invisible"; they see the folks walking by pretending they are not there. We can never allow this to happen in our hearts. We are ignoring Jesus when we ignore the poorest members of society. We are neglecting an opportunity to take the faith in our hearts and translate it to action. Check out these words from the **Book of James**:

What good is it, my brothers, if someone says he has faith but does not have works? Can that faith save him? If a brother or sister has nothing to wear and has no food for the day, and one of you says to them, "Go in Peace, keep warm and eat well," but you do not give them the necessities of the body, what good is it? So also faith itself, if it does not have works, is dead. (Jas 2:14-17)

There are numerous other Scripture passages for us to look at here. The most brutally challenging comes from **Matthew** in **chapter 25**, where Jesus informs us that whatever we do to or for the least members of society, we do to him. Jesus literally makes our response to the poor salvific! So, our response to the poor is not just a nice bonus, but essential to our place in heaven someday.

I wanted to include a section from the **catechism** here, but had trouble picking one. The problem is that there are more than 50 listings in the **catechism** referring to our need to be charitable people. That in itself is a message. More than a message; that is a challenge.

Be generous today. Give to the beggar. Volunteer at the soup kitchen. Work at your local shelter.

Take your faith and put it into action.

Warning! Bad joke ahead!

I heard a great story about a photographer who was assigned to take pictures of a waterfall. He was advised that a small plane would be waiting to fly him over the site.

The photographer arrived to find a small Cessna airplane was waiting. He jumped in with his equipment and shouted, "Let's go!" The tense man sitting in the pilot's seat swung the plane into the wind and soon they were in the air, though flying erratically.

"Fly over the waterfall and make several low-level passes," the passenger said.

"Why?" asked the nervous pilot.

"Because I'm going to take pictures!" yelled the photographer.

The pilot looked terrified while asking, "You mean you're not my instructor?"

Chapter Four: Questions about issues of the day

Dear Fr. Joe,
Why is the church so opposed to euthanasia? Why is it wrong to alleviate suffering? It seems to me we demand more compassion for a suffering dog than a person.

Thank you for your question. I know this is a hard issue to look at and sometimes it may not seem to make sense. I hope this column helps. What I intend to do is take a look at the topic of euthanasia and give some of the reasons why the church does not support this idea.

Intellectually, we have to look at the context of euthanasia. Too often, we make an assumption that there are no medical alternatives to allow us to "die with dignity." Now, I do not have the time or expertise here to cover all of the alternatives. So, I encourage all of you reading this to research those medical options including pain management and hospice.

As a side note here, I also have to say that in a day and age when we lack faith in people, it amazes me that we would be so comfortable giving an entire class of people the power of life and death over us.

Philosophically, euthanasia presents a problem morally from the standpoint of what is called the "slippery slope." The slippery slope argument points to the tendency of power to corrupt. Once you give people (and not God) power over life and death, it tends to corrupt the individual. It seems OK for us to "assist a person in death" who expressed a desire to die, but then we could move to "assisting" those who have expressed no desire, but who we think would want to. The next step is, obviously and tragically, ending the life of those we feel should want to die.

When we look at the many and varied abuses that occur in the health system now, can we honestly say we trust them with the power to say who lives and who dies? This is NOT a rip on doctors, nurses and other people who help us stay healthy and alive. This is a tragic statement of reality about the current health care system when evaluated in light of trends we have seen throughout history.

Spiritually, we have a whole other set of problems when looking at euthanasia. We make, as far as I can see, two assumptions in supporting euthanasia that do not line up with our Catholic tradition and faith. First, we assume that suffering is always bad. Secondly, we assume that we have the ultimate power to run our lives.

Is suffering always bad? Starting with the premise that we were saved by Jesus' suffering and death, I believe that we can state the answer to that question with an emphatic "no." I remember giving a presentation at a church where I was approached afterward by a man who indicated it was easy for me to be happy and have faith in God because I hadn't suffered. I asked him if he considered the possibility that I was happy and had faith because of intense suffering. He didn't see it.

What a shame that we cannot see that there is a value to suffering that encompasses the whole person. We learn much about ourselves and the world around us in our pain; we also learn what joy is, don't we? How would we know the goodness of happy moments if we didn't have pain? I know from experience that people assume if you are happy in life, you have never suffered. What a tragedy. Again, lacking the space to explore this issue in depth, I ask you to consider what I am stating.

Secondly, we assume that we have the power of life and death over ourselves. Good news, folks, we do not. God created us to love and serve him in freedom. By freedom, I do not mean doing whatever we want to do. That leads to slavery to our desires. The only place we will find freedom is in our surrender to living the way we were created to live – as God's own children. A part of that involves surrendering to God and even joining him who suffered so greatly for us. I have written in the past about this concept of "joining our sufferings to Jesus."

I want to close with a reflection on the phrase "dying with dignity." I vaguely remember the first time Jack Kevorkian took someone's life. I can recall all the news coverage and how he left the dead person in a van outside the county morgue. I also remember, as the number of his victims climbed, his casual attitude about the whole thing. Finally, I remember the *60 Minutes* episode where he euthanized someone for a television audience. I did not watch the show (and have boycotted *60 Minutes* since then), but in the news the next day, the comments were that Kevorkian asked the "patient" if he was ready, then said "Okey-dokey" and poisoned the man. I don't see any dignity there.

I know this is a difficult topic, and I assure you I have had to deal with it in my own life with loved ones. I have found great strength and hope in the teachings of the Catholic Church and pray that you will experience this as well.

Warning! Bad joke ahead!

I got this one over the Internet from an eye doctor: I was performing a complete physical, including the visual acuity test. I placed the patient 20 feet from the chart and began, "Cover your right eye with your hand." The patient read the 20/20 line perfectly. "Left." Again, a flawless read. "Now both," I requested. There was silence. He couldn't even read the large letter on the top line. I turned and discovered that he had done exactly what I had asked; he was standing with his hands covering both eyes. I was laughing too hard to finish the exam.

Chapter Four: Questions about issues of the day

Dear Fr. Joe,

How should we look at the war on terror? I am not clear on our role as "peacemaker" when we are fighting. What is peace?

Is it just me, or is that joke about the eye chart a great analogy for Catholics in America, wrestling with Catholic social teaching and the war on terrorism? I am going to do my best to present what the church teaches.

Let's go to the *catechism*. There, we find peace defined as one of the fruits of the Holy Spirit mentioned in *Galatians 5:22-23*. *(CCC 1832)* Peace is a goal of Christian living, as indicated by Jesus who said, "Blessed are the peacemakers, for they shall be called children of God." *(CCC 1716)* The fifth commandment requires us to preserve and work for peace. I also like St. Augustine's definition of peace: "the tranquility of order." It is "the work of justice and the effect of charity." *(2304)*

So, we see that there are two levels to peace – personal peace and social peace.

Personal peace is something we find within ourselves even when everything around us seems to be in conflict. I once heard my sister Laure use a great analogy. In science class, Laure learned that when a storm hits the open seas, the fish that normally swim close to the ocean's surface dive deeper into the waters, because the depth is constant even when the ocean's surface is going wild with wind and waves. This constancy at the depth, Laure said, is her idea of the peace that Jesus gives.

Peace, I believe, lies within our hearts. We do not have to go and get it; it was instilled within us at our baptism. It is the depth to which we go. You have felt this peace – in fact, I would guess that there have been times in your life when finding that peace within you caught you by surprise. No matter what happens around us – or even to us – we know that Jesus conquered sin and death for all time. Because of this, we are more than conquerors. *(cf. Rom 8:37)* *John 16:33* states,

> ... *In the world you will have trouble, but take courage, I have conquered the world.*

Let's keep that idea in mind as we look at our current situation in the world. We can find personal peace no matter what is going on around us.

The next idea is more difficult to explain in light of our current war on terrorism. The *catechism* breaks down how a Christian should act in time of war in *sections 2302-2317*. These are very important sections – check them out.

According to the *catechism*, it is our duty to avoid war "because of the evils and injustices that all war brings with it." We must not enter into conflict out of anger or hatred. People who renounce violence to defend and protect human dignity show real Christian ideals to the world " ... provided they do so without harming the rights and obligations of other men and societies." *(CCC 2306)*

However, the church teaches that in the current state of the world, governments must be allowed to defend themselves once it is clear that more peaceful methods will not work. Because of the severe nature of war, the moral reasoning for it must be clear and well-founded.

In *section 2310*, we learn that soldiers in the military are servants who protect the common good and maintain peace, provided they act honorably and out of duty. The government must respect conscientious objectors, provided they opt to serve human dignity in an alternative way.

So, what should a faithful Catholic do during this time? I believe that the only way to honor the clear requirements of the church during this time is to develop a well-informed conscience.

How do we form a well-developed conscience?

First of all, I think we must work hard to purify our motives. Our thinking and our actions cannot be motivated by a hatred or love for the current president, by racism, by a desire for vengeance or even by complacency. We must, in all things, be motivated by a desire to achieve true peace in the world and protect and defend human dignity. Social peace is not possible without the presence of justice.

Once we have purified our motives, we must learn as much as we can about the current situations. Read and research; listen and converse with people who have served as a compass for you in the past during times of questionings and wonderings.

Obviously, during this process, we must pray. Pray that God will pierce our hearts with the light of truth. Pray that God's will be done in our hearts and in the world. Surrender the situation to Jesus and ask him what your role is to be in this conflict. I sometimes catch myself saying, "Well, all we can do is pray," which is kind of like saying, "Since we can't do anything else, we may as well pray." But prayer is the start and the finish of everything.

Once we have done this, we must act on our conscience. That part is easy. The second requirement is a little more difficult. We must trust that people around us are following their consciences, too.

May God bless our efforts.

Chapter Four: Questions about issues of the day

Dear Fr. Joe,
Is it a sin to join the military if the war is unjust?

This is a tough one and a bit nuanced. Let's see what we can do with it.

Often in these musings of mine, I will point out how we need to form our conscience in union with the church and its teachings. In this case, as polarized as we are politically, it is particularly important that we look to the church for guidance in order to keep from "baptizing our politics."

When you speak of an unjust war, then, let's look at the church's standard for what is a just war.

Our wisdom on this comes primarily from St. Thomas Aquinas. You can find it in your **catechism in section 2309**, which states this:

The strict conditions for legitimate defense by military force require rigorous consideration. The gravity of such a decision makes it subject to rigorous conditions of moral legitimacy. At one and the same time:
- *The damage inflicted by the aggressor on the nation or community of nations must be lasting, grave, and certain;*
- *All other means of putting an end to it must have been shown to be impractical or ineffective;*
- *There must be serious prospects of success;*
- *The use of arms must not produce evils and disorders graver than the evil to be eliminated. The power of modern means of destruction weighs very heavily in evaluating this condition.*

The evaluation of these conditions for moral legitimacy belongs to the prudential judgment of those who have responsibility for the common good.

What we are to do with this information, then, is place it in our hearts, listen for the church to make a declaration about whether the war is just or not, and then pray for the wisdom to follow it.

If the church has not spoken, you will need to follow your own conscience about whether or not you believe the war in question to be unjust or not.

People who join the military do so for numerous reasons: some require the vast financial assistance available to them if they join; others seek training in fields that will provide them with a lifetime of skills which will feed them and their families. Other people join to grow in discipline and or "team concept." There will also be those noble persons who join the military out of a sense of duty and gratitude.

Whatever the reasons, if someone joins the military during a time of "unjust war" in order to provide assistance in a non-killing manner, I believe that to be morally acceptable. For instance, priests who serve as chaplains in the military do not necessarily need to agree with the war to believe that their help is desperately needed. Medical doctors, or those in training to be doctors, may feel that they are called to offer their skills to soldiers in a war that they believe to be unjust or that the church has deemed unjust.

Dear Fr. Joe,
Can I be a conscientious objector?

Not until there is a draft...OK, bad joke, sorry.

Absolutely. I can find no teaching from the church that says you have to join or accept draft into the military, even if the church declares a war just. In **section 2311**, the **catechism** states:

> *Public authorities should make equitable provision for those who for reasons of conscience refuse to bear arms; these are nonetheless obliged to serve the human community in some other way.*

So, that much is clear. We know that if an individual feels called to be a conscientious objector, he or she is not just allowed to follow that prompting but is actually required to do so.

Let's pray and work for peace.

Dear Fr. Joe,
Should we really be celebrating holidays such as Christmas when so much of the world is at war or otherwise suffering?

That's a great question! It's important for us to be aware of what is going on in the world and be sensitive to that. So, what does Christmas say to the events of our time? How do we celebrate the holidays, when our world is deeply troubled?

So what should we do at Christmastime? We should celebrate. We look the idea and the season of Christmas right in the eye and see how it applies to our world. So, let's dive into the moments of Jesus' birth and life.

Jesus was born around 3 B.C. in Israel. At that time, Israel had been in a state of perpetual warfare since the time of Alexander the Great. The

Romans had occupied Israel and had set up a puppet Jewish king who slaughtered his own people. The Jews were searching for freedom, and were fighting among themselves as to how to deal with the Romans. The religious leaders were ideologically divided on important issues. This was the time that Jesus was born into: political, social and religious turmoil. God could have come into this world in any country at any time in history, yet he chose one of the ugliest. Think about that. Wouldn't you agree that our need for Jesus has rarely been as obvious as it is now? It's the perfect message for us in these times.

Celebrate the fact that Jesus loves us in the midst of our unloveliness. Celebrate that he didn't wait for us to call on him; he came and called us. What a concept to celebrate! So the next time Christmas rolls around, as we wrestle with issues like warfare and fear, terrorism and anger, understand that Jesus wrestled with these things, too. At our worst moments, Jesus wants to be with us. So, we who are dealing with the same issues as the people of Jesus' time know that Jesus dealt with these issues too. And he emerged victorious.

Now, by saying he emerged victorious, I don't mean that he drove the Romans out; quite the contrary. One of the things that Jesus taught us is about how to be free during a time like this. How do we act as a people of freedom? First, we can let go of hatred and anger in our hearts. We are experiencing the same pains as the Jews of Jesus' time and when Jesus spoke to them, he spoke of loving enemies and forgiving each other *(see St. Matthew's Gospel)*.

Second, we can let go of our worry. In **Matthew, chapter 6**, Jesus points out that none of us adds a day to our life span by worrying. He said that if our Heavenly Father looks after the birds of the air and beasts of the forests, how much more will he take care of us?

Third, we can refuse to be enslaved by fear. Jesus said, "Do not be afraid; just have faith." *(Mk 5:36)*

Fourth, and most importantly, Jesus reminded us to "Remain in my love." *(Jn 15:9)* Whatever we do, wherever we are, whatever the situation, we must keep in mind that we are loved by the author of love.

God intervened in human history to save us, to walk with us and to show us how to live and love. We can be confident that whether we live or die, we are the Lord's. *(Rom 14:8)* You and I are God's special possessions. Scripture says that we are the apple of his eye. That love is something we can be confident of and take comfort in. Much more so than fear, we are surrounded by the love of a God who comes to us at our darkest moments and sees the best. Celebrate that, brothers and sisters.

Dear Fr. Joe,
I have to make a decision between sending my child to Catholic school, which would involve me going back to work full time, and staying home with my younger children who are not in school yet. What do I do?

Great question! What you have here are two conflicting goods: Catholic education and being home with your kids. The good news is, no matter what you decide, a good thing will happen, right?

So, what do we do?

In my mind, there is nothing I can think of that would trump you staying home with your children. I believe that that is an invaluable experience for your young ones, and I can't imagine any circumstance where that good should be neglected.

The fast-paced nature of our country and difficult financial times have often pushed parents into making tough decisions financially, and I don't want to be insensitive to that. I remember that quote from *The Screwtape Letters*, by C.S. Lewis, where a senior devil says to a student tempter, "If I can't make them bad, I'll make them busy." And that seems to be a huge factor today. I will focus on the benefits of Catholic education and offer some alternatives for those who simply cannot pull it off financially.

When I think of my experience at a Catholic school, I find it difficult to articulate how important I feel a Catholic education is for one simple reason: Jesus. As a Catholic, there is nothing more integral to our human experience than the person of Jesus. At a Catholic school, we can introduce Jesus into every element of the students' lives.

When a student needs help, we can pray. At my Catholic high school, when we have experienced tragedy, each time, our response (at the student's request), has been to have Blessed Sacrament exposition.

A part of the life of a student at a Catholic school can be daily Mass, confessions, prayer, all on top of learning. I honestly believe that there is nothing better than that.

I also point to our teachers at Catholic schools. As a general rule, teachers at Catholic schools are taking a serious financial hit. They could make much more money elsewhere, but choose to minister in their role as a Catholic school teacher. That kind of sacrifice touches my heart and introduces a powerful element into the education equation. Usually, our Catholic schools don't have the financial resources of our public schools and we struggle with our facilities and the opportunities we can offer, but I think that if we continue to strive toward being faithful to the teachings of Christ and his bride, the church, we will grow to be all we can be.

I'll close this section with a quote from our bishops who say that Catholic school education offers the "fullest and best opportunity to realize the fourfold purpose of Christian education, namely to provide an atmosphere in which the Gospel message is proclaimed, community in Christ is experienced, service to our sisters and brothers is the norm, and thanksgiving and worship of God is cultivated." *(Renewing Our Commitment, 2005)*

Now, despite the obvious benefits of a Catholic education, some simply can't do it. There are a couple of things to do here that may help – and again, we are going on the premise that the most important thing here is the possibility of being at home with your children.

First, have you considered home-schooling? More and more Christians are taking this option and finding a great opportunity to combine the power of family time together, traditional education and a strong faith life. There are numerous resources available on this issue and I encourage you to check them out. I would bet there are any number of people in your parish who are practicing home schooling and finding it to be a great joy. Also, I know that many groups who are home schooling are combining their resources and working together.

I think another thing for you to consider is your parish religious education program. I think a lot of people overlook this incredibly valuable opportunity to help their children grow in faith and knowledge. Make sure and check with your parish about the opportunities available to you for religious education programs for your children.

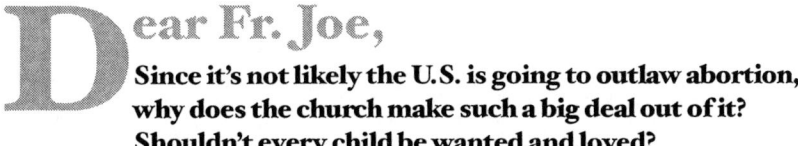

Dear Fr. Joe,

Since it's not likely the U.S. is going to outlaw abortion, why does the church make such a big deal out of it? Shouldn't every child be wanted and loved?

Thanks for the question; this is such a big issue. Let's get right to it.

According to the church, the abortion issue is the biggest moral issue that we deal with as a country. We know abortion to be the taking of innocent human life, and there is no higher crime than that.

Let's look at some of the reasons we consider abortion to be "The Issue."

No one really attempts the old argument that "it's not human." Have you noticed that? The argument surrounding the abortion issue has now been framed as "the right to choose."

That's a terrifying reality, and we need to think about that. The right for a human to exist in this country is now reduced to a choice. The inability of human beings inside the womb to express their will to live is the chief reason they end up dead. When we reduce human existence to the choice of another, we have done a terrible thing.

Another reason we reject abortion is that since we are talking about a human, we are talking about the sin of murder. Murder is one of the "Big Three," and God absolutely and always forbids it.

We oppose abortion for many other reasons also, but I would think those listed above would be sufficient.

So, why make a big deal out of it? Because in the United States, we have to. Nearly 25 percent of pregnancies in this country end in abortion. This is a crime of the highest magnitude.

In addition to the children being killed, the women who procure these abortions often end up victimized. Years of therapy and a great deal of love and forgiveness are the only cures for women in this position. If and/or when we encounter women who have been victimized by abortion, it is essential that we treat them with gentle love and the forgiveness and mercy that God shows us. Condemnation will not help; love will.

Although it is important to keep the hope alive that eventually the United States will outlaw abortion, too much focus on that hope can at times be a distraction from our primary mission: to work hard as God's people so that until that time when it's no longer a legal option, it's not perceived as a necessity.

We can do this through our loving offers of help to those women who are in need. We can open our homes to these young women. We can sign up to adopt if we are in a position to help, we can volunteer at pro-life organizations – so much we can do.

Because our help is so desperately needed and because of our Christian missions, we simply have to "make a big deal out of it." God has called us to be people of life, standing up for the weak and those who have no voice.

When we act on behalf of human dignity, we must always treat people with human dignity. Killing or attacking anyone in the name of life is not only the definition of irony, it is a sin. Jesus treated even his enemies with respect for their dignity and we must do the same.

In terms of politics, abortion is not an "equal" issue. It's the big one. Since the numbers of the slaughtered are so high and the need for conversion so desperate, this issue needs to take pre-eminence in our voting. All of our Catholic leaders have spoken on this and we simply must allow that message to permeate us.

Chapter Four: Questions about issues of the day

Our attitude, not just our politics, must be pro-life. People who know us should know without asking that we are not simply "anti-abortion," but actually "pro-life." The way we talk, the way we act — it's all gotta scream "I am pro-life."

We must be strong on this. Future generations will weep for the destruction we've wreaked on the world here and ask us about our silence. We simply cannot afford to "let this one go."

Pray for the grace to stand for life.

Dear Fr. Joe,

I'm thinking of going into politics someday. Am I obligated to assure that my political opinions all reflect the church's teaching exactly? What if I disagree about something such as abortion or the use of our military?

I think it's wonderful that you are thinking of going into politics. As much as we joke about politicians and are often saddened by the public sins of some politicians, there is always the possibility and call of public service done in the spirit of Jesus.

You should make sure to be preparing yourself for this great and noble calling. Begin now reading all that you can on the Catholic Church's teachings on social justice. Your *catechism* has a great many teachings on who we are called to be and this can be your guide.

It's a sad reflection of our country that the Catholic Church is often criticized for "using its influence" to tell politicians how they should vote. I believe that the official way to respond to that kind of statement is, "That's garbage."

No one tells people that their family or their upbringing shouldn't affect them as politicians until it conflicts with what they want their politicians to do. The fact is, if our faith is not an integral part of our lives, then it's not faith, it's something else. The church has a right and a duty to share its wisdom with its children. Our faith is a 2,000-year-old faith that has existed in every culture in the world during that time. We've done some incredible and beautiful things and we've made some terrible mistakes. Add that to the guidance of the Holy Spirit and you'll find that the church might have some great wisdom to share with us in our decision-making.

When we get to abortion, we're hitting on one of those subjects where there simply is no wiggle room. The church says that the right of every human to exist can never be reduced to the choice of another person. On this issue, there can be no compromise and no equivocation; abortion is immoral and a crime and we can never support it in any way, shape, or form. When we get to the issue of war, if the church tells us it is an unjust war, then the same principle applies for the same reason: the taking of a human life is always a huge issue for us, as every person in the world has his or her God-given dignity.

The Web site *http://www.ewtn.com/library/BISHOPS/capolvot.htm* has a great article from Bishop Michael Sheridan on the duties of Catholic politicians. He starts off strong and it only gets better; I highly recommend reading it.

Due to space limitations, I'm just going to quickly summarize the beginning of his article, share a couple of his great quotes, and then ask you to read the rest on your own time.

One of the key points Bishop Sheridan makes is the idea that our well-formed conscience is to be our highest guide and that the phrase "well formed" is an important one. A well-formed conscience is tied to objective truth and must always be in union with the good that God wills and has been given through natural law and divine revelation. Our own judgment cannot be placed higher than that.

Sheridan next points us to **number 2302 in the catechism**, which states:

...to the church belongs the right always and everywhere to announce moral principles, including those pertaining to the social order, and to make judgments on any human affairs to the extent that they are required by the fundamental rights of the human person or the salvation of souls.

He then states:

When Catholics are elected to public office or when Catholics go to the polls to vote, they take their consciences with them. Pope John Paul II has consistently taught this as, for example, when he said that those who are directly involved in lawmaking bodies have a "grave and clear obligation to oppose" any law that attacks human life **(Evangelium Vitae, 73)**. *The Congregation for the Doctrine of the Faith has declared that, "in this context, it must be noted also that a well-formed Christian conscience does not permit one to vote for a political program or an individual law which contradicts the fundamental contents of faith and morals"* **(CDR "Doctrinal Notes on Some Questions Regarding the Participation of Catholics in Political Life," 4)**. *Anyone who professes the Catholic faith with his lips while at the same time publicly supporting legislation or candidates that defy God's law makes a mockery of that faith and belies his identity as a Catholic.*

Let's pray that our Catholic faith is always reflected in our actions: "your light must shine before others, that they may see your good deeds and glorify your Heavenly Father." *(Mt 5:16)*

Dear Fr. Joe,

I always feel so much pressure at Christmas time. There's so much that has to be done and I have to make sure I get the right gift for each person. How can I balance my perspective so that Christmas is the prayerful experience it is meant to be?

Many of us may experience the same kinds of pressures in the Christmas season. We get ready to take a big bite out of the season and enjoy what God has cooked up for us, but we find that in the end, all we've got is cheap, dry hamburger bun. I mean, hey, when it's that time of the year, we are running around like crazy. Now, just to be clear, this isn't going to be one of those "You are missing the reason for the season!" lectures. I figure we have enough guilt over other things that we don't need any more. Let's face it: at Christmastime, we've got shopping to do!

How do we do the shopping, the running, and handle the seasonal craziness and still stay focused? That is the big question. Before I answer it, though, let me give a disclaimer: We're going to talk about money, and the one thing we have to remember is the need to be financially responsible. Our money is a gift from God and we always need to be thoughtful in how we spend. Got it? Good. Now, let's get to the meat of our discussion on Christmas.

It's a natural tendency on our parts to be worried about taking Christmas gift giving to an extreme. Some have even said that we need to dump the whole gift exchange practice, so we can go to the "real meaning" of Christmas. But I think we have to ask ourselves an important question: What if gift giving IS a big part of the real meaning of Christmas?

Here's what I mean:

Christmas recalls the day of Jesus' birth. We celebrate the fact that God took flesh and walked among us. God became one of us in order to save us. THAT is God's gift to us, and the greatest gift we will ever receive. We celebrate these two realities by giving gifts to each other. First, we give gifts to Jesus by using all he gave us to glorify God. Secondly, we give gifts to Jesus by loving his people and celebrating the presence of God within them.

Thirdly, we give gifts to Jesus by giving gifts to his people. For instance, there's that sweater you gave your brother last Christmas (you know the one: that real ugly green-and-red number with the flashing lights). Jesus dug it and says "thank you."

Do you see what I mean? We don't have to feel guilty for running around like crazy people, buying presents for those we love, because it is a way of expressing our thanks to God when we do it responsibly. So, the next time Christmas rolls around, in the midst of your shopping, offer it all as a prayer. You'll find Christmas more rewarding, gift giving more exciting, and the whole season will be a time of celebrating God's love for us and our love for him and his people. And you just might decide not to buy another ugly sweater, too.

Warning! Bad joke ahead!

A really nice family from the parish invited me to dinner. As I entered the house, the couple's young son grabbed my hand and led me to the table. He was very excited. As we sat down, the boy's father said, "Who would like to lead the prayer before dinner?" The youngster's hand shot up and his dad said, "OK, son, but remember, pray like you have heard Mom or Dad pray." The son nodded solemnly and bowed his head saying, "Oh Lord, why did we ever invite Fr. Joe over tonight?" Oh well ... at least the food was good.

Dear Fr. Joe,

At work, they are replacing people with machines. Is that moral?

That is a tough one. Try this one on for a safe answer: sometimes it is and sometimes it isn't. Let me explain. When is it moral? When it is necessary. When it does not violate the dignity of the human person or undermine the contributions of a safe working environment. In 1891, Pope Leo XIII wrote an encyclical, *Rerum Novarum*. In it, he said that it is the obligation of the worker to show up, work hard and honestly and provide for his or her family in an honorable fashion. The same document gives a much longer list of responsibilities for those who employ workers. Among those obligations are to provide dignified labor, a just wage, safe working conditions, freedom to attend Mass (or other Christian services) on holy days of obligation, placing the dignity of the person above the value of money.

Replacing people with machines can be wrong if people are being replaced simply so a few individuals at the top can make more money. Echoing Pope Leo XIII and the church's social teachings, the ***Catechism of the Catholic Church*** states,

> *Those responsible for business enterprises are responsible to society for the economic and ecological effects of their operations. They have an obligation to consider the good of persons and not only the increase in profits. Profits are necessary, however. They make possible the investments that ensure the future of a business and they guarantee employment. (CCC 2432)*

The responsibility of employers is a serious matter. Jesus refers to this, saying,

> *Much will be required of the person entrusted with much, and still more will be demanded of the person entrusted with more. (**Lk 12:48**)*

On a personal level, I'd thank all of those who work so hard to provide for their families. If you are one of the people who benefit from someone's hard labor and commitment, please be sure to thank them with all your heart.

When we work, we praise God. We use the bodies and minds that God gave us and we provide for ourselves and our families. We make available to the world products that are needed. There is no way to overstate the value of hard work.

Whatever we do, let's dedicate the fruits of our labor to God. Don't forget that one of the ways we can thank God for making our work possible is by being sure we tithe to our local church.

Warning! Bad joke ahead!

The other day, I was at the airport and saw none other than Microsoft billionaire Bill Gates. I was there to meet someone and thought I would play a fun game. I approached Mr. Gates and told him I was meeting someone I would like to impress. I asked if he would wait until my friend got off the plane, and then approach me and act like we are friends. I couldn't believe it when he agreed. So, my friend got off the plane and as we were greeting each other, up walked Bill Gates! As my friend stood there, mouth agape, Mr. Gates said, "Fr. Joe! What a pleasure to see you here! We haven't talked in so long!"

I looked at him and said, "Back off, Gates, I'm trying to say hello to a friend."

OK, maybe that didn't really happen, but it is a great joke ...

Dear Fr. Joe,

What's the problem with software piracy? If it's possible to do it, why is it wrong? After all, Microsoft has billions – it's pretty much a victimless act.

The first thing to look at is the idea of equivocation. When we equivocate, we make two basic statements, such as the following:

"We never run in the hallways, unless we are on fire." (I have some experience with this rule).

See how an equivocation works? It gives you a rule, then an exception. Now, let's look at the commandment, "You shall not steal."

Now you notice what's missing from this commandment? Equivocation. Stealing is always wrong. When God gave us that commandment, he didn't say, "unless they are rich" or "unless you really need or want it." God simply says, "Don't steal."

Besides the "no-equivocation" nature of the commandment, there are more reasons why it is wrong to steal and then say "Well, the other person has more money." For example, let's look at it this way – you are rich. You may be sitting there thinking you're not, but as far as 90 percent (not an official number) of the world are concerned, you are shockingly rich. Does that mean that people from other countries are allowed to steal from you? Of course not!

So, in the same way that we would never like that principle applied to us in our situation, we should never apply it to others. Besides, I talked to Bill Gates in the airport yesterday and he said he needed the money.

Basically, software piracy is wrong because God said not to steal. It's just that simple.

Now, I don't like to pile on any more than the next guy, but let's look at some things that are stealing that we may not have thought of, such as cheating on a test or paper. This is stealing. Cheating is taking someone else's work and calling it our own. If you don't do your work assignment, and the gal next to you stayed up late doing it, you are stealing from her if you copy it. This applies to taking credit for work we didn't do at our jobs, as well as to schoolwork.

Check out these numbers, parents. *(http://archives.cnn.com/2002/fyi/teachers.ednews/04/05/highschool.cheating/index.html)* We have to do a better job when teaching our kids about stealing/cheating:

- A national survey by the Rutgers Management Education Center of 4,500 high school students found that 75 percent of them engage in serious cheating.

- More than half have plagiarized work they found on the Internet.
- Perhaps most disturbing, many of them don't see anything wrong with cheating. Some 50 percent of those responding to the survey said they don't think copying questions and answers from a test is even cheating.

Another thing we may not have thought of in regard to stealing is giving money to the poor. Yup, folks. Believe it or not, not giving of our money to help out those who need it is stealing. Throughout the Old and New Testaments are references to the importance of believers setting aside a tenth of their income to give to their church or to the poor. The reasoning behind this is simple: God gave us the gifts and talents we have, and those gifts and talents are what allow us to work and make money. One way God has asked us to thank him for those gifts and talents is to help out our brothers and sisters in need. When we fail to do that, then it is just like stealing.

So, in the end, we once again find that God believes the best of us: He believes that we can make it in the world by being men and women of character. Our focus can be really simple: we must never steal.

Warning! Bad joke ahead!

My sister Edie is a mother of three, and these three are a source in my life of unending joy and humor. Recently, she has begun compiling a list of things she hears herself saying to her children that she never thought she would say, like this comment she directed at 5-year-old Christopher: "Christopher, put the iguana down during family prayer time."

Dear Fr. Joe,
Are any great scientists Christians?

There are tons. Ready for this? The author of the Big Bang Theory? A Catholic priest. It's true! "But Father," you may say, "how is this possible?" It's very possible. We must never be afraid of knowledge. If it is true, then it will teach us something about God. Here is an example. Although the Big Bang Theory may contradict the words of *Genesis*, it does not contradict the message of the creation account in *Genesis*. What is important about the creation account in *Genesis*? Six days? Rest on the seventh? What happened each day? The order of creation? No. What is important is that a loving God created everything out of nothing and only for reasons of love. God created us in his image.

These facts are what make the Jewish/Christian account of creation unique from any other creation accounts.

Einstein said that if the Big Bang occurred, the odds of it being random are similar to that of an explosion occurring in a print shop that resulted in a complete set of encyclopedias. It just ain't gonna happen.

For more amazing Christians in the world of science, check out Blaise Pascal, Sir Isaac Newton and Copernicus, to name just a few!

Warning! Bad joke ahead!

During my time in the seminary, I was assigned to a parish that was, shall we say, on the wrong side of the tracks. I found the parish completely surrounded by big, high barbed wire fences and an alarm system that could wake the dead. Gunfire and sirens were the order of the day – and night – as we tried to sleep. I felt right at home.

Around my second week there, I was sitting on a bench in front of the parish when a young man approached the fence and called to me. He was coughing loudly and trying to tell me something. Naturally, I was concerned. I went over, opened the fence and led him to the house where I got him a glass of water. He finished the drink and stopped coughing. I asked, "Are you OK? What were you trying to say?"

At that point, he pulled a gun out of his pocket and said, "Give me your money."

Dear Fr. Joe,
Thinking back on the TV coverage of Hurricane Katrina, the media showed a lot of people stealing from stores and other places. Given the circumstances, was that OK?

Wow – good question. Let's start the answer by looking at the Scriptures; no better source, right? We read ***Exodus*** and find that the seventh commandment says, "You shall not steal." Seems pretty straightforward, right? Well, maybe. One of the words we have to pay attention to in that commandment is "steal." What does that mean exactly?

According to another great book, the ***Catechism of the Catholic Church***, stealing is "unjustly taking or keeping the goods of one's neighbor and wronging

Chapter Four: Questions about issues of the day

him in any way with respect to his goods." The key question is this: Do we think the victims of the hurricane were unjust in taking things they needed to stay alive? Common sense, charity and the church all tell us the same thing – no.

Ownership of property is a gift – we are simply stewards of the things we own and we're supposed to use our gift to benefit our brothers and sisters. Obviously, in a case such as the hurricane, it should be our desire to help those people who are in desperate need. If we don't want to share, then we've got our priorities out of whack.

According to the *catechism*, theft is

usurping another's property against the reasonable will of the owner. There is no theft if consent can be presumed or if refusal is contrary to reason and the universal destination of goods. This is the case in obvious and urgent necessity when the only way to provide for immediate, essential needs is to put at one's disposal and use the property of others. (CCC 2408)

That's pretty clear, right? Someone who is starving is not stealing if they take food.

On the other hand, stealing a TV is a different story – it's not an immediate, essential need, especially when there's no power!

Dear Fr. Joe,
How do I witness to my Catholic faith without being called a Jesus freak?

That's easy. Don't mention Jesus.

Sorry, I had to do that. I love this question. I hope we know not just that we have to witness to Jesus, but witness well. So, how do we do that without being called a "Jesus freak"? I don't know that we can. I think persecution for loving God is inevitable. In fact, I think that if we aren't being harassed about our faith, we may be doing something wrong.

Our lives must be about Jesus. Our school, our work, our family – everything about us must proclaim the truth of the Catholic faith to the world. A warning, though: the world won't like it.

Look at the *Gospel of John, chapter 1*. The world does not like the light. The letters of John makes this clear, as well. Heck, look at what happened to Jesus. Do we think that anything different will happen to us for proclaiming him?

The first step, then, in effectively sharing our Catholic faith is to accept that some are not going to like it. Some people will make fun of us, shun us or even work against us because of our decision. We must remember the words of Jesus that we are blessed when we are persecuted for him.

Once we understand this simple principle, there are certain things we can do in our sharing of our Catholic faith that will help us be effective. We don't do these things to avoid suffering. We do them to make sure that our witness is one people want to follow. How do we do this? Here are some of my ideas:

We must be authentic. A lot of people equate acting phony with being Christian, and that is not it. Be who you are and who God created you to be. God knew what he was doing when he made you with your personality. Don't crush it because of false ideas about piety.

Discern when you should speak and when you shouldn't. A lot of times, our silence will speak better than a speech. If we see a wrong action, or hear something inappropriate, a lecture may not be the appropriate response. People not laughing at stupid or sinful things I've said have challenged me more often than a long discourse on the decay of Western morals and civilization.

Be honest in all your dealings. Don't give any person a reason to be scandalized by cooperation with evil. If you proclaim yourself a faithful follower of Jesus and the Catholic faith, then people will be watching you closely. We must be men and women of character and never give anyone reason to say or think, "Well, Joe is a Christian and he did it."

We will make mistakes. We will, at times, go overboard, or slip in moral situations. There will be times where the witness we present will be more harmful to the kingdom of God than helpful. When we fail – notice I didn't say "if" – we must ask God's forgiveness and seek to make right whatever needs to be made right. Don't get discouraged! God's love and power is bigger than our sinfulness and failings. People who proclaim their Catholic faith and fail at times are not hypocrites. They are known as "Catholics." Catholics sin; sick people need a doctor – it's the same thing.

Be informed, knowledgeable people. Know why we teach and believe the things we teach and believe. God doesn't often ask for blind faith. We can be informed, intelligent, faithful followers of our Catholic faith.

All that I have said is a tall order, isn't it? Clearly, we are going to need divine help. Don't forget to pray and ask the Holy Spirit to strengthen and guide you.

Now, get out there and live your faith!